This book is dedicated to my Aunt Moira who sadly passed away while I was on the trip. I will never forget you.

Preface

You will become aware very quickly that I am not so much a literary man, more of a mad keen motorcycle adventurer who loves to record and share his story. I hope you enjoy coming on the journey with me.

I longed for an adventure and the universe delivered.

The Idea

"Don't wait until that mythical time to ride the Americas" I wrote in my book, *Ride to the Midnight Sun* in 2012. Did that spark something in my subconscious? Did I issue myself a challenge? I'm not sure, but gradually the thought of riding from the bottom to the top of the planet became very appealing.

On April 23rd 2013 I received a text from my friend Wilson, asking if I was at home and fancied meeting for a beer. It was unusual since Wilson lived in Zurich, Switzerland and I would normally be working in the south of England on Tuesdays. At this point Wilson was on a business trip to Glasgow and I happened to be working from home, and agreed to meet up in Glasgow city centre for a few beers and a bite to eat. It was a pleasure to be heading off to meet an old friend rather than spending my evening in yet another hotel, as would be my Tuesday night norm.

I met Wilson at Queen Street station, just off Glasgow's George Square. We had been meeting at regular intervals since getting re-acquainted after a twenty-year break, and this time headed off to the famous old Glasgow pub, the Horseshoe Bar for some real ale. It was not long before the talk turned to motorbikes. I had recently returned from a one-week bike trip in South Africa with another friend Raymond, and Wilson was keen to hear all about it.

Moving on from the Horseshoe Bar we ended up in Jamie's Italian restaurant in George Square where we started enthusiastically discussing future trips. Completely unplanned, I asked "Why don't we ride around the world"? to which Wilson responded "What I really fancy is to ride the Pan American Highway". "Actually", I replied "that is the most appealing trip I have on my radar". It's a three-month trip unless you're Nick Saunders, the crazy record breaker who rode the route both ways in under forty-nine days. Assisted by more red wine we quickly got to the point where we both raised our glasses and agreed "let's do it". We would ride south to north from Tierra del Fuego in Argentina to Prudhoe Bay in

Alaska. We would plan for 2016 to give us time to prepare, save and give notice to our wives. It was an exhilarating feeling.

Next day we were back at work, but the commitment I had just made was at the forefront of my mind. Any spare moment was spent on Google researching the route. It looked like the best way would be to ship the bikes into Buenos Aires and ride down to Tierra del Fuego. From there we would ride all the way up through South, Central and North America to Prudhoe Bay in Alaska, then turn around and ride south to Anchorage to ship the bikes home.

I have to admit I felt overwhelmed at one point and needed to check in with Wilson to make sure he was still committed. I sent him a message asking are you sure? It's at least 3 months; we could do North America instead? The response was clear "I want to ride the Pan American Highway, South to North and that's it". It was the perfect response and gave me the confidence that we were really going to do this.

Wilson agreed to my suggestion to invite Raymond, who lives in Australia. As I mentioned earlier Raymond was also up for bike rides having just been with me to South Africa, though this was a hell of a bike ride. I emailed him with our plans and was not surprised when he replied the next morning with "absolutely up for it".

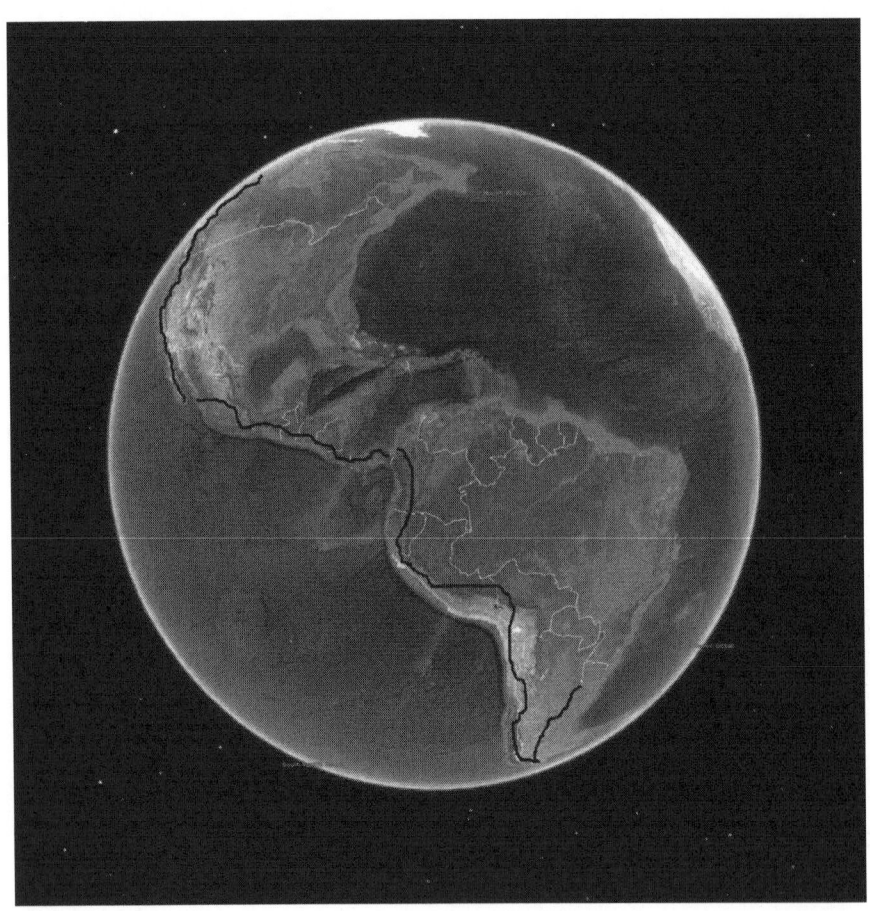

"The route heading north"

Who are we?

We are all in our fifties and I live with my wife Amber in Lenzie near Glasgow, Scotland. I have a daughter, two sons and a step daughter. I was working as an IT consultant travelling mainly to England on a regular basis. Raymond is married to Joyce has two sons and lives in Sydney, Australia. Wilson is married to Yvonne and has a son and a daughter. He returned to live in Stirling, Scotland recently after spending 14 years living in Germany and Switzerland.

I was raised in New Cumnock, a little mining village in South East Ayrshire. My father was a Colliery Electrician and later a trainer. My mother worked in various part time jobs but qualified as a nursery nurse in later life. I grew up with my older brother in a two-bedroom council house in the schemes (estates) that had been built to house the predominantly coal mining work-force. I was very average at school, not helped by my refusal to wear glasses, despite being quite short sighted. That no glasses decision was sparked by a kid called Roger Austin who chanted Joe Ninety at me. Staying on at school beyond 16 never entered my head. It was very rare for anyone from our village to go on to higher education. With 4 O-levels (one B and three C's) it seemed totally natural for me to leave school at 16 and find a job.

My first real job was in a menswear shop where my brother also worked. I moved from there after a year or so to another more local menswear shop where I hoped it would somehow become less tedious. Sadly, it was not.

By that time, I was passionate about motorcycles sparked by seeing a wealthy kid turn up at school on a Puch sports moped. I managed to get my parents to give me a loan of £100 to buy an old BSA Bantam which I first rode legal on the morning of my 17th birthday. I still remember the excitement as if was yesterday. That BSA proved to be very unreliable and was eventually replaced with a second hand Honda CB125. Much more reliable but I wrote it off against the side of a minibus after my friend

"Wee Fernie" clipped me from the rear. Then came a new Honda CG125 which I held on to for a couple of years.

It was during the CG125 period I spied a couple of shiny bikes sitting outside the house across the road where my friend Billy Jess lived. I could not resist going over to take a look, and was seduced by a gorgeous shiny red Suzuki GT185. As I was circling the bikes two boys came out with Billy. One of them was Raymond and another was a boy named Cliff Paton. Initially Raymond had been concerned I might be stealing or damaging his bike but we hit it off straight away. He had just recently bought the little Suzy and was keen to go for ride outs. He was a year older, lived in Cumnock and worked at a Carpet shop in Kilmarnock. We started going out on the bikes and soon formed a strong friendship with many teenage exploits over the next few years. Raymond lived in a big old rambling house in Cumnock. His father worked in Stationery sales and his mother ran their home.

Both of us were very disillusioned with our jobs and were seeking something better. I told Raymond I had heard about an American Computer company that had opened just outside of Ayr and sounded like a great place to work. The company was called the Digital Equipment Corporation. After one failed attempt I managed to secure a warehouse job. Raymond had already been hired as a trainee mechanical assembler. It proved to be a very wise move as it sparked what turned out to be great careers for both of us.

Wilson, who is three years younger than me, also joined Digital a few years later as a mechanical assembler. I cannot exactly recall how we first met, but it was probably in the motorbike shed, and again we hit it off straight away. Wilson lived in a village called Annbank and his father worked on a farm shared by several brothers. His mother was then a housewife but later became a great telesales pioneer for a double glazing company. By the time I met Wilson, there were a few of us all bike crazy, working and playing hard.

I am prompted to tell the story of our upbringing in response to some negative feedback on my first book *Ride to the Midnight Sun* from someone called Butch. I get the feeling Butch had me down as a spoiled rich kid taking my modern BMW on a biker's holiday. The truth is we all came from stable but humble beginnings and we have all worked hard and done pretty well. We were also all lucky to join a young and progressive industry; I will always be grateful for that chance to join Digital.

The working and playing hard continued for a few years. Our final act before re-uniting in later life was a visit to the Isle of Man TT in 1980. As usual I suffered mechanical problems with my by then rebuilt write-off Suzuki 250X7 while the rest of the boys had good quality reliable machines. It was towards the end of that holiday we had a 'handbags at dawn' confrontation over some beer that had been thrown around. I think that marked the start of the group of us drifting apart. Wives, kids, divorce and all the usual life events took place over the years and some of the boys spread their wings and left Ayrshire.

The road to reunion began with a conversation between my friend Jim Kerr (the Moose) and me. He told me he had met Raymond Danton (Big Honda) our mutual friend from the past who had been over visiting from Australia, where he now lives. Around the same time Wilson (Hutch) had also made contact with me. I asked the Moose if he had contact details for Raymond and he gave me an e-mail address. I emailed Raymond and sure enough he quickly replied. This was followed up with several mail and Skype conversations where we very quickly re-connected our lives.

I have always felt a strong attraction/connection to the USA South West since I first travelled there to work in the 80's. I fell in love with the scenery, the history, the culture and the food. In fact, it was on one of those trips that I picked up the Moose at Albuquerque airport as he flew in for some meetings. I will always remember the Moose walking towards me dressed in a denim jacket and jeans. I think this was his attempt to recreate the Cowboy look. He came over all macho (not his normal demeanor) saying the long trip was a breeze and insisting that he should drive. He pushed me aside and marched straight to the car and got in. Only one issue, he had chosen the passenger side. I sat beside him in the driver's seat and smiled.

"OK you drive - and get that smirk off your face" he said.

It was during these visits I used to look with envy at people on motorcycles, especially those who were on a road trip. I would walk around the hotel car park at night ogling the bikes.

I guess inside my head I connected up all of this, the nostalgia of meeting up with friends after all these years, our passion for motorbikes and a place that I loved and was accessible for all.

On the 19th of September-2009 I wrote

Gents,

Most of us are more than half way round in terms of life expectancy. Big Raymond's down under and the rest are spread around up top. I propose we meet Half Way Round for a beer. Having had some fantastic trips with the Moose, a great night with the Hutch and after some beer fueled discussions re Harleys and the USA

I propose the following.

We meet in Phoenix in Apr or May 2011, hire Harley's (or what you fancy) and spend a 5-7 days touring the Southwest. Weather is highly likely to be great, motels are cheap, Beer is cold and we have lots of time to get good flight deals.

Possible route

Phoenix - Flagstaff - Grand Canyon - Santa Fe - Albuquerque - Las Cruces - Tucson - Phoenix

Yes, we will have Jet Lag

Yes, it's not a long trip for the travel involved

Yes, it will be brilliant

Please let me know if you are interested with any suggestions you may have. I appreciate you may have other commitments (work, family, finance).

I do not have a mail address for Big Tree. Does anyone have it? Have I missed anyone? Not sure if Fred the Swordsman will have a mail address :<)

Cheers

Stephen

The replies came fast and furious and soon we had Honda from Sydney, Hutch from Zurich, Moose from Irvine, Scotland and Honda's younger brother Stephen (Pup) from Cleeve, England signed up. Very shortly after we had tracked down and signed-up Ian McCrorie (Big Tree) from Cumnock as our sixth and final member. Tree advised us that he never had a full motorcycle license so he would opt for a convertible instead. The Moose and Pup decided they would share with Tree. So that left us with 3 bikers and 3 in a car.

We named the trip the Tupp Inn Reunion (Out Loose wae a Moose IV). The Tupp Inn in Cumnock used to be the meeting point for our Motorcycle club. We would meet there in the late seventies for a pint then a blast usually down to Ayr. Bikes ranged from 125 – 750cc and we had a characterful bunch of members. I can still remember the line of bikes outside the pub and that fantastic feeling as we snaked through the Ayrshire countryside. Why Oot Loose wae a Moose IV? This came about in 2007 when I met the Moose after an almost 10-year break. We decided after a few beers we should take an overnight trip up north on the bike. We were as good as our word and arranged a trip to Skye the following May. We had a fantastic time and have been doing it every year since.

Lots of communication took place over the next period from idea to reality; key points included the commitment of credit cards to flights and hotels. The ultimate financial commitment came from Big Honda with his purchase of a brand new BMW Motorcycle to allow him to get re-acquainted with bikes. We had an itinerary so we knew where we were sleeping each night but routes and stops would be up for grabs on the go. Close to departure the convertible idea was dumped and replaced with a 4x4 which was much better from a luggage carrying point of view.

In the final few weeks I talked to Tree and Moose on the phone arranging a meet-up time at Glasgow Airport of 6am.

"We'll be having a dram before we get on the plane" Big Tree announced.

"Er Yes" I replied, wondering what to drink at 7am?

Guinness I decided, that's good for you.

The trip turned out to be excellent and this was followed up with a couple of "Oot Loose wae a Moose" trips to Plockton in the highlands with a sub-set of the team. A further major trip to Northern California for all six participants was arranged for May 2014 (OLWAM VII).

In 2012 I embarked on my biggest bike adventure to that point and that was a solo trip to the most northerly point of mainland Europe: The Nordkapp in Norway. I wrote a kindle book titled *Ride to the Midnight Sun* documenting why I believe you can turn any trip, no matter how short, into an adventure. In 2013 Raymond and I decided to do a "Meet half Way" Tour which was a week-long bike tour in South Africa. We once again had a fantastic time and both agreed it had been the best experience of biking roads to date.

The Long Wait

A lot of time was consumed on the web looking at different equipment options. Many Skype calls were made and much debate ensued on the right type of bike. I planned to take my trusty 2009 BMW R1200GS called Boris, Wilson had a notion for a GS Adventure but wanted to see the new 2014 version and Raymond considered a smaller bike such as the R800GS. The debate around big, small, used, new was to continue for some time.

I guess the earliest form of real preparation came with the launch of Motoscotland which is an off road school run by Clive Rumbold in Inveraray. Off-road training was something I always wanted to do so when the chance of a fairly local outing came about, I jumped at it. Wilson was also very enthusiastic when he heard about it and booked it while on holiday in Scotland a few weeks before I was due to go. My booking happened to coincide with a visit to the UK by Raymond who joined me. All three of us had a great experience with it. Raymond and I followed up the Introduction course with the Foundation one a week later, just before he set off home to Australia. With confidence gained from the introduction, we were having a fantastic time riding the trails around Inveraray when the other guy on the course Derek took a fall. I was right behind him, so able to quickly dismounted to check if he was ok. He said he was fine but when he removed his helmet an extremely nasty cut above his top lip was revealed; it went all the way through the tissue. He was a hardy oilman and claimed he was good to go, but I had to insist he sat there until the others returned. Clive and Raymond soon turned back, and Derek was taken to the local clinic at Lochgoilhead some 20 miles away. Our day finished early. Clive contacted us soon afterwards and agreed we would get another half day 'on the house' at a later date. Derek made it to the clinic and was soon sorted out and looking forward to having another go at some point.

A couple of months later Wilson's mother's unexpected death brought him back to Scotland. I remembered Jenny fondly from our young biking days. En route to the funeral I took a detour past their old house in

Annbank. I sat for a while pondering on all the activity around the house with bikes coming and going. Wilson's dad Wullie had aged but still looked great. I promised him I would come down and show him my bike. I had booked a banked half day off to be spent at Motoscotland at the end of that week and I decided to ask Wilson if he fancied joining me. I thought it might help to get his mind off things. He immediately accepted and we had a great day, the only blip being me falling off on a steep descent. More practice required I decided.

On presenting the trip plan to Amber I had suggested that she might visit me at some point on the journey as it was going to mean quite some time apart. This conversation came back up during one of our red wine chilled Saturday evenings. She sensed I had an issue and in her typical style probed me to find out what it was about. She was right of course and the issue was that I was feeling as if a visit from her during the trip would create some kind of break in the flow of the trip, and take more co-ordination between us riders to organise. She did not really get that at first, but did when I said it would 'domesticate' my adventure. We left it that night but she came back to it and said that it was a thirteen-week trip and she had agreed to it thinking we would get together sometime during it. More importantly, she felt it had been her way to feel part of the adventure. I got that, and agreed she should join us somewhere. In the meantime, I had contacted Honda and Hutch to check on their plans. Honda's wife, Joyce, is a teacher and we would be travelling during term time; Hutch had not made arrangements with his wife Yvonne yet. I told them I would take a few days out in the USA and would catch them up, and both were fine with taking a planned break at that point.

Reading became a big part of the preparation. I read the blog of Pat around the America's (Barcelona Pat), Gobblers Nob, Leprechauns in South America, The Longest Ride and Tortillas and Totems.

In November 2013, BMW launched their new 2014 GS 1200 Adventure at the Milan bike show. Wilson was living in Zurich and was close enough to go visit. He soon had a deposit down on one, for delivery in March 2014. Raymond read the press release from Sydney and soon became convinced that this was also the bike for him. I must admit I did like the look of it via the web but did I need to spend so much on a new bike when Boris was perfectly capable? The only doubt I had was driven from bad memories and past experience. When we were boys I always had crap bikes in comparison to Wilson and Raymond and this came to the fore when my Suzuki X7 (built from a write-off) kept breaking down on our Isle of Man TT visit in 1980. I shuddered at the thought of my, by then seven-year-old, bike giving me problems. At the same time Boris had been totally reliable, had crossed the Arctic Circle before and was fully equipped for the task. I decided to wait and at least see what the new Adventure looked like in the flesh, maybe test ride it, but my heart was still firmly with Boris.

Wilson and I had some discussions about using our trip as a fund raiser for a charity. We decided we would just each do our own thing, making individual charity choices. One evening arriving home from work, I noticed a brochure had been delivered outlining Deafblind Scotland's campaign to raise funds for a purpose built centre on a field they had purchased very close to my home. The campaign was called the "Field of Dreams". I knew straight away that this was the charity for me. I contacted the charity and arranged to meet Drena the Initiatives Officer.

Drena could not have made me feel more welcome and was buzzing about our trip. Apparently she had some opposition to the location of the centre from people living in my street. The fact that I actually lived in the street was just the icing on the cake. In March of 2014 Wilson and I and our wives attended the Deafblind Scotland Gala Ball where we presented our plans for the trip to the gathered throng. A few weeks later we met up with Drena in her office where we also met Stephen Joyce, who is registered deaf and blind. The task was to explain the charity and what we were doing to some visiting school kids from Lenzie Academy; they were working on a competition for charity funding. I was totally humbled by Stephen's story told with Drena using sign language. Stephen is completely deaf and has severe tunnel vision which he was able to demonstrate to us through a special pair of glasses which shows what this would look like to sighted people. Stephen works at Deafblind Scotland travelling solo by train each day. He has also climbed Mount Kilimanjaro and since that meeting has completed the three peaks challenge in the UK. What a guy. Stephen carried a Deafblind Scotland banner on his journeys and later presented it to Wilson, for us to carry during our trip. We were very proud to take it with us.

We also met John that day, who is also registered deaf and blind, and who enthusiastically showed us pictures of a Norton he used to race. It was really funny when he revved Wilsons bike slightly over enthusiastically out on the street.

I had previously made attempts to pull the trip forward from March 2016 to March 2015. I was thinking, why wait? Let's get on with it. Raymond had been keen on this too, but Wilson was not willing to commit to it as he was in the middle of trying to arrange a move back to Scotland from Switzerland, and had just started a new role in HP. He wanted things settled, to ensure Yvonne was comfortable with the pull-in. A turning point on the date was on Friday 29th of November 2013 during a Skype conversation. Wilson declared he had sold his house and bought a new one in Scotland. He now felt that the pull-in was a good working assumption, and would confirm by March 2014. This was followed up by an email from Raymond who was on a business trip in India confirming that not only was he up for a possible pull-in, he was excited about it. Wilson and Yvonne had also decided at that point that Yvonne should fly out while we are in the USA to spend some down time with Wilson.

Not long after that Wilson advised me he had decided to leave HP and take a career break. Based on that March 2015 became the official trip departure date. Wilson's decision on time out was an interesting one, as I too had struggled lately with my travelling, a high pressure lifestyle, and I had almost decided to do the same earlier in the year. I started off in my travelling IT consulting role at 40 saying I would do it for five years. I had by then been doing it for fourteen years. I had re-set my goals to say I would make a change at 55, which was coming up in May 2014. I had then reset that to October 2014, five months before our big trip. A combination of some frustrations at work, seeing Wilson make the brave move, and a deep desire for change helped me make the decision to resign from HCL on May 9th 2014. That was one day before my 55th birthday. I was clear I was not retiring but taking some time out to travel and consider my options.

On Monday May 12th Wilson and I set out on Boris and Ludwig (his new GS Adventure) for a camping trip in the highlands. We headed up through the Cairngorms then took the North East Coast road to John O' Groats. From there we followed the coast road to a campsite in Durness. The weather was sunny and we pitched our tents in the prime spot on a small outcrop overlooking the ocean with beaches on two sides of us. We lit a fire and drank some Highland Park whisky with a solo German biker Thomas, who was pitched nearby. Next day we travelled down the West Coast (one of the most scenic routes on the planet) and pitched up at another fabulous site in Applecross. This had been Wilson's first experience of camping in many years and despite having stayed in some fantastic hotels with superb views, he had to admit our £7 views were way beyond value for money.

Next up on the agenda was "Oot Loose Wae a Moose VII. This was a Northern Californian route that had been 3 years in the planning. All the original participants' attended including Hutch, Pup, Honda, Moose, Tree and I. Honda, Hutch and I hired BMW 1600's, while Pup hired a Honda Pan European or at least the US equivalent. Tree and Moose hired a 4x4 that could easily accommodate luggage and passengers when required. The route took us from San Francisco down Pacific Highway 1 to Morro Bay. From there it was East across the hot central belt to Yosemite National Park. This was followed by "the finest ride" from Yosemite over the Tiago Pass to Lake Tahoe. From Lake Tahoe we headed east to Napa Valley and then finally crossed the Golden Gate Bridge back into the Bay area.

The trip was fantastic and I was very impressed by the BMW. The handling, sound and power was incredible for such a large sports touring bike. The trip also gave us a chance to get used to riding together and try out our Scala Rider Communication systems. Although fiddly to pair up, once connected they proved to be a fantastic purchase. It also gave us an opportunity to manage conflict which occurred on a couple of occasions and for sure would feature in the big trip. As usual there were many great laughter moments during the trip but my highlight was when Big Tree (an undertaker by trade) produced a silky coffin pillow on the plane to rest his head on. "Perks of the job" he said with a smile. He offered it to me half way across the Atlantic which I un-politely declined.

Hutch and I booked up for the UK HUBB event held at the Donnington Farmhouse Campsite right next to the famous race circuit. The HUBB (Horizons Unlimited) is a forum that was created by Grant and Susan Johnson. It was a mainly motorway route down to the event but the bikes were comfortable and the Scala's relieved the boredom. The event itself was excellent. A bunch of likeminded people camping together with some vendor stalls, entertainment and adventure rider presentations. The weather was perfect too. We bumped into Barcelona Pat while waiting in the café queue. Barcelona Pat did our planned trip in 2009 and his website has been both inspirational and useful in our preparations. Pat was a quiet, likeable Welshman and was happy to join us for lunch, then take us to show us his bike, Idris. He readily answered our questions about the trip. A recurring theme seems to be the nightmare of the Patagonia winds.

I wanted to get flights booked as soon as they became available. Initially I had been checking one way flights to Buenos Aires. These had been coming in around £700 which I though was steep. I then decided to try and see if I could get a return with split locations. I could not find anything with a return out of Anchorage but did find Glasgow to Buenos Aires, Vancouver to Glasgow with KLM and at a great price of £708. I emailed the others and they agreed we should go ahead. Honda would first fly to the UK a week or so in advance, and travel with us. With that I made the booking, and committed the first of our budget. Departure would be 28th Feb 2015 with a return on the 13th Jun 2015. We had expanded the original 3 months (13-week plan) to 15 weeks to accommodate the planned visit by our wives and to give a little contingency. Theoretically we could change the flight dates for £100 if a similar fare was available. This was an exciting moment as it made things feel very real.

Shortly after that I received a call from Wilson to say he had spoken to a Travel Insurance company and he had a great deal for cover for our trip. The company was Navigator Travel Insurance and the premium was £156. It was the same company Barcelona Pat used. We went ahead and booked it.

We also finalised our choice of shipping agent selecting MotoFreight based in Egham. An obvious choice had been James Cargo used by many others but to be honest I was very unimpressed by their lack of response to my communications. If they can't call me back, how can I trust them with my bike? MotoFreight had been advertising in Adventure Bike Rider Magazine and the response from Roddy was swift and comprehensive. They would pick up our bikes in Scotland a few weeks before our flights and aim to get them there the day before we arrive. They advised us they would use Dakar Moto in Buenos Aires to assist us clearing the bikes.

Barcelona Pat had also mentioned that we should check vaccinations well in advance. We took his advice. I arranged an appointment with our local nurse and she laughed when she saw my list of countries. She advised me I needed Yellow Fever, Rabies, Hep B and Typhoid. Luckily I was already covered for Hep A and Tetanus. I was surprised to learn that the vaccinations would cost over £300. Still, you have to have them, so I kicked off the six-month process with my first round of jags.

In late August we booked the "lassies" flights. Both Amber and Yvonne would fly out to LA to spend a week with us assuming we made it on time. Surprisingly these flights cost more than ours. I reserved a hotel in LA using points I had accrued in my working life. This established the second hard deadline for our trip, the first being the flight home.

Wilson had mentioned the trip to Alan Dalziel, the manager at Parks BMW Motorrad in East Kilbride, and asked if they might be willing to contribute to Deafblind Scotland. Alan had been quite enthusiastic about it and said he thought that he could drum up interest within the Parks Group. Various emails and conversations took place and finally Alan came back not only with an offer of support for Deafblind Scotland but also tyres, oil, servicing and spares for us. In return he wanted us to route our blogs via Parks website, attend a winter dealer event and display their logo on our panniers. To be honest, I was initially a little uneasy over this in relation to my concept of a fully self-funded trip. I thought it through and what I meant by a fully funded trip was that every penny raised for Deafblind Scotland would go to Deafblind Scotland. This was still the case, and of course the additional support for us would be very welcome.

On the bike preparation front I finally made a decision on panniers, which would be my biggest bike accessory expenditure. This decision making process took me over a year. Keep the plastic BMW panniers, buy top of the range Touratech or UK made Ardcase all swilled around in my mind. The decision was finally made during the HUBB trip where I spotted one bike with a set of Bumot panniers. They looked stylish and solid. The bike belonged to our proposed shipping company MotoFreight. I asked the owner and he was very enthusiastic about them pointing me towards the Adventure Bike Rider website. On returning home I found out they were manufactured in Bulgaria and the reviews were positive. I ordered a set which included a cut-out for the exhaust and a tool box. Delivery took around two weeks but the wait was well worth it. I loved the style and quality. Fitting was hindered by having no instructions, so I called the Adventure Bike Shop which was closed that day. I then tried calling the manufacturer Assen, who despite being on holiday managed to mail me a link from his hotel. Very good service indeed. I later bought the inner bags which again were great quality. They had a much stronger frame than the original BMW panniers, and felt very robust. The capacity was also greatly increased.

Raymond decided he would finish up work at Xmas, which was a bit earlier than he had planned. In late September Wilson and Raymond had a conversation that resulted in a proposed pull-in and extension of the trip. Instead of leaving at the end of February they proposed we leave near the beginning. The logic was that now that we had a hard commitment to meet our wives in LA we did not want to feel as if we had rushed South America. Raymond had also received some very good feedback about Bolivia which was a country that was not on our list.

My first reaction was one of surprise. I knew there had been some spousal tensions around the length of the trip as it was. I also wondered what the financial impact of changing tickets and insurance might be. Regardless I saw the benefits and ran the proposal by Amber that night. She, as expected, was supportive whilst we both acknowledged this was a long trip now getting longer. As the planning man I did the research on the changes and after some coming and going with KLM, managed to get the flights changed to the 2nd of February for the basic £100 change fee. The travel insurance was also straight forward but took us into a new bracket due to length of stay, thus cost an additional £60. I also informed MotoFreight and Dakar Moto in Argentina (the fixers) who both responded positively.

While communicating with Dakar Moto I took the liberty of asking them for a suggestion for our first night hotel stay. They suggested a few, including the Posada de las Aguilas hotel next to the Ezeiza Airport where the bikes would be shipped to. I booked that, and at the same time negotiated a pickup from our arrival airport (AEP) some 30 minutes away for $45. As we were arriving at 10:20pm I did not want to mess around with taxis and directions.

So the outline plan as agreed with Roddy at MotoFreight and Sandra and Javier at Dakar Moto was as follows.

2nd Feb – Bikes arrive

2nd Feb – We arrive

3rd Feb – Bikes are cleared

4th Feb – Depart BA (or maybe stay an extra day for sightseeing)

My goal was to get us travel ready ASAP then make decisions on when we actually departed.

It was now mid-October and only eighteen weeks from departure. Amber and I continued to discuss contingency plans on what she might do in the event of various problems. Simple things like if the washing machine breaks down does she fix it or replace it, through to major issues i.e. what if one of my parents were to die. We were both aware this was now quite a long trip, and it felt quite strange and emotional at times. Wilson and Yvonne and Raymond and Joyce were also dealing with emotions around the length of the trip. In reality, I agreed with Amber it is a long time, but felt it would be all over in a flash. A flash of brilliance, I hoped.

I had now been finished with work for five months. It had been a fantastic summer being at home, great bike trips and lots of dry weather. I had put more mileage on Boris during this period than any other motorcycle in my life. The old boy was now topping 26,000. With winter approaching I started to reach out for possible short term work assignments with the first point of contact being my old company. I was getting "we need you" calls from my ex colleagues but the decision maker was not making it happen. I was unclear if it was demand, politics around re-hiring employees as contractors or something else. My options were fairly limited as most contracts last at least 3 months with possible extensions. My hard stop of mid-January would be a barrier.

I had a coffee with Graham O'Neill who worked as a contractor on a project I was on a few years before. Graham is also a biker, riding the very impressive 1400 Kawasaki. Graham was excited to hear about the trip and admitted to feeling a bit envious. I discussed the contracting market and my situation. He agreed getting something with a 16-week deadline would be almost impossible. He did however think that the fact I had taken a year out to do what I am doing would in no way detract from getting a contract on my return. In fact, if anything he thought it could be quite a positive story to tell. On the same day I received a mail from my old company saying that they have a policy of not re-employing leavers as contractors until 24 months after their leaving date. It looked like it would be post trip before I would be working again.

November passed quickly with Hutch and I attending a Deafblind Scotland lunch in Glasgow. It was there they announced that a benefactor had left them over £500,000 in his estate which was fantastic news. We also attended the Motorcycle Live Event in Birmingham followed by a visit to the National Motorcycle Museum. We had a fantastic time both agreeing the new Ducati Scrambler was the star of the Motorcycle Live Event and the Brough Superior was the star of the Museum. We also took our panniers in to Douglas Park Motorrad to have them blinged up with Douglas Park Motorrad stickers.

I noticed in the forums that there were another few Brits on the road in the Americas. They included the Two Wheeled Nomads (Lisa Morris and Jason Spatford) who are living an alternative life from their bikes. Lisa connected with me on Facebook and regularly posts interesting updates. Jason's video work was outstanding. Maybe we could catch up with them on our way north.

A significant milestone occurred on December 8th when both Boris and Ludwig were uplifted by Parks. The next time I got to ride Boris would be in Argentina.

I started to talk to Amber about plans for the short seven weeks we had left. Unlike me she does not plan years or even months in advance. She was feeling a bit emotional as we talked it over. At this point we had the normal festive activities with the kids coming back and forward. For Hogmanay we had booked the Edinburgh street party and overnight accommodation. That was a first for us and we were looking forward to it. After that we had the Parks event on January 13th. This event would be exclusively for Deafblind Scotland and us. This was to be followed up two days later by the bike collection (MotoFreight). On a personal front I had booked a table for Amber and I at Glasgow's Grill on the Corner on the 24th of January. I also arranged a farewell event the final Saturday for the kids. I still had to arrange a boy's night out including Raymond, and a farewell visit to my parents. My parents visit felt as if it could be an emotional one, with both being in their eighties. Them worrying about me, and me worrying about them.

On Wednesday the 18th of December Wilson and I had a mechanics day at Douglas Park Motorrad. We were hooked up with their main man, Stevie Cowan. Stevie serviced Boris while we watched and learned. It was a fantastic experience. That night I posted on our new Facebook page.

9am: Couldn't put a nut in a monkey's mouth

5pm: Senior BMW Technician

The new Facebook group was part of some hard work from the previous day where I had upgraded our website and Justgiving page. Douglas Park Motorrad had also created a page on their website for us. This certainly seemed to spur on some further donations to Deafblind Scotland. On Thursday the 19th of December we broke the £1000 mark.

Xmas proved to be fairly relaxing, with the family coming and going. For Hogmanay Amber and I went to the Edinburgh street party. A first for us and to be honest, probably the last, as it was mobbed, disorganised, with queues round the block for the loos, and lots of impatient drunks. Still the fireworks were the best I had ever seen.

As 2015 began I reflected on how glad I was that we were going at the beginning of February rather than March. With deep snow on the hills I was feeling a bit of cabin fever setting in and I just wanted to get on with it. I think my restlessness was getting to Amber; irritation was setting in.

Then I got myself into a bit of a tizzy over my computing choices. I had planned to take my 3-year-old IPad with a keyboard, then suddenly felt this was a problem, with a lack of storage space for video. I spent hours researching alternatives and decided that I needed the new top of the range IPad Air 2 with 128GB of storage. I was uncomfortable though, as not only was it expensive I would need new accessories such as camera sim connector and keyboard. I questioned Amber whether she thought I needed a keyboard or protective cover and she asked, do you really need anything new? That next morning I listened to a podcast on Adventure Biker Radio with a guy called Rene Cormier. Rene advised never to buy anything close to the trip departure as it's highly likely to be a fearful purchase. He is absolutely right, I thought. That day I cleaned up the files on my existing IPad, creating space. I was sure if I kept moving my files onto the cloud this would work just fine. It turned out to be a wise decision as a friend of Wilson's, who worked for Acer, was later to provide us with a netbook each.

Wilson and I did our final mechanics day at Douglas Park. This time it was new rear discs and semi off-road tyres for both bikes. The tyres were Karoo 3s provided by Metzler, arranged by Alan at Douglas Park. The Metzler representative, Iain Duffus, was in the showroom at the time. He was really pleasant, and we thanked him for his support. He had commented that he wished he was coming with us, to which Wilson jokingly replied "are you a mechanic?". It was only later that we discovered Iain was a former motorcycle racer, and had in fact won two TT's. (Junior and Super sport). He was also second five times and third two times. I am sure he is also an excellent mechanic. I was gutted I had not had the chance to talk to him about it, but we at least had the chance to say thanks.

The bikes were now valeted and ready to go. They looked fantastic perched up on the motorcycle lifts. We absolutely loved the whole mechanical training experience. We had formed a great working relationship with Stevie and Scott the mechanics and their apprentice Paul. There was a lot of good Scottish humour going on between us by now.

Another exciting January event was when Wilson discovered that a ferry service had started up between Columbia and Panama avoiding the infamous Darien Gap. The Darien Gap is an undeveloped swampland between Columbia and Panama that is less than one hundred miles wide but dangerous and impassable unless you have guides and winching equipment. Most bikers have been airfreighting their bikes across but this is costly and often the service is poor. The thought of a cheaper option that allowed us to stay with our bikes was really appealing. Prior to this a sailing option meant hitching a lift on a yacht which sounded fantastic, but the realities of the bikes lying on a deck and incomplete customs paperwork was not appealing.

I did a little more research and found the ferry company name FerryXpress. I made contact with a guy called Robert Kong who had commented on their Facebook page. Robert had taken the ferry from Panama to Columbia and was very positive about it. He was less positive about Panama which he described as unfriendly. As always people experience countries in different ways, depending on many factors such as their own nationality, culture and personality. I decided I would judge them when I got there. He did sing the praises of Columbia though, and he expected our experience to be even better coming from that direction. He also hooked me up with a Pan American travellers Facebook page covering all types of transport i.e. foot, peddle, engine etc. We agreed we would try and meet up down south if our paths crossed. He even offered us accommodation in northern California. It felt good to have the first chance human encounter with another adventurer.

A week before our customer event at Douglas Park, STV Glasgow confirmed they would cover it. They would interview us and Deafblind Scotland. The local paper the "Kirkintilloch Herald" also interviewed me for a short article. This was all good news for the charity fund, which had now grown to over £1600. The night before the customer event STV Glasgow pulled out stating they did not have a reporter available. I was mightily pissed off, as I had set expectations with Douglas Park and more importantly the charity. They suggested an in-studio interview just prior to leaving, but I had little faith in it happening.

I woke up to a cold and snowy January 13th with a forecast predicting more snow and tricky conditions around evening commute time. This was not going to be good for the customer event, from a numbers point of view. I decided to go early, and take the equipment we were shipping with the bikes stored in the panniers. We had decided to take as much as possible as check-in luggage as the goods going with the bikes would be uninsured. In the end I took the tools, tents, bike covers and a few camping bits and bobs to ship with the bikes. The staff from Douglas Park were eating Indian carry out when I arrived and they greeted me like one of their own. I must admit I did feel very comfortable in the shop wandering around with no boundaries. I appreciated the trust they showed in me.

First to arrive for the event was Carina Cairns and her friend Lynn. Carina is an enthusiastic Biker granny originating from Switzerland but now living in Edinburgh. I had met Carina via the Central Motorcycle Meet-up group and we had always gotten on very well. Carina bought a BMW bear and had me sign it like a celebrity. More people started to arrive including my children and their partners and my close friends Big Tree and the Moose. Raymond's wife Joyce also attended with her friend. She was over visiting her mum and Wilson had the great idea to invite her. We hoped it would give her a different perspective on the trip. Amber had a work appointment that night and said she would try and make it if the roads were ok, but she would arrive late. It was a strange feeling to be at a public event like this where I featured on a personal basis rather than work.

Drena, Stephen and Christine arrived from Deafblind Scotland. We quickly updated them on how the presentation would flow, and we were ready to go. Alan Dalziel the manager at Douglas Park kicked off with a welcome and passed across to Wilson and me to do our stuff. I was delighted to see Amber arrive just as we kicked off. It all seemed to go really well with a mixture of facts and humour. The highlight for me was Stephen Joyce from Deafblind Scotland. Stephen, who I mentioned earlier, is deaf and registered blind although he has some tunnel vision sight left. It was great to be able to let Stephen tell his story to the assembled bikers. There were a few questions after, then just some general one to one conversations as people gradually made their way home. Just before we left a gentleman named Iain McLeod came over to Wilson and me and said he would donate one thousand pounds. We were astonished and delighted and thanked Iain for his generosity. Apparently Iain makes a substantial donation to charity each year in memory of his late wife. There are some good people out there.

The following day Wilson and I and his dad met up again at the dealership. The mission this time was to collect the spare parts that were being provided and decide what should go with the bikes and what we would take home. In the end we packed away most of the stuff with the bikes but took home oil and tyre inflation cartridges which would be classed as hazardous. When we picked up the spares we realised we did not have any additional brake pads. We decided we would order a set of pads for each bike and an additional air filter. This would see us through the first 12,000 miles or so. We ordered them from a company called Motorworks who we have found to be very reliable and provide good value for money.

The bikes were picked up by Motofrieght as promised on Thursday the 15th of January and I received a confirmation from Roddy that they had them down in Egham ready for crating. He joked about how clean they were at this point. I agreed I don't think Boris has ever been as clean since new. Paul at Douglas Park had done a spectacular valet job. Roddy also advised me that he would have to return the BMW puncture kits as they were hazardous and he would also return our keys which he duly did.

It was quite ironic my bike was in Egham as that was the UK base of my most recent employer HCL. Many a night had been spent late in that office churning out proposals fuelled by pizza. It was only eight months ago, but seemed like a different life. I still dreamt about work a lot, and pondered with some level of anxiety what I would do post trip. I was certainly not retired as such; I would do something, but what?

It was at this time we had also decided on a late change to tyre strategy, Raymond had been raising a concern over the availability of tyres and was suggesting we take a set with us. To be honest we had expected a spare set from Douglas Park but did not argue when it turned out not to be the case. I made some enquires and Javier from Dakar Moto advised that tyres for our size of bikes were not easy to get and were very expensive.

However, he was of the opinion that our current set would last to Lima, Peru where he had an excellent contact for tyres. I asked Javier if he would keep tyres and ship them to us at some point but didn't get a clear response. Both Raymond and Wilson were now of the opinion we should buy tyres, ship them with the bikes and carry them. I was concerned about carrying them as they would be heavy, bulky and liable to theft. However I did agree we should take them. After some hurried phone calls to Roddy at Moto Freight, and a 24-hour delivery internet tyre order, we were the proud owners of the recently launched Michelin TCK70's. They had reviewed well and apparently would give better mileage than our Metzler Karoo 3s. We were in the perfect position to assess the results. Hopefully we now had enough rubber to get us to at least Mexico and maybe LA? I posted a question on the Pan American travellers Facebook group asking if anyone knew of any companies that would store and ship tyres but there was no response. It looked like we were all going to be carrying our spare tyres.

Raymond set off for the UK on Wednesday 21st of January; his son posted a photo of him at Sydney Airport on our Facebook group. Effectively as a team the journey had begun. I met up with Raymond on the Friday to take him shopping. True to form he was later than expected and got lost in Lenzie. I always find it strange seeing him in the flesh after all these months of Skype and email conversations. He was remarkably fresh having just arrived the night before. He said his hello to Amber, then I quickly whisked him away to Firecrest Motorcycle Outfitters in Glasgow.

This shop is located in an industrial estate just off the M8 motorway and is run by a young enthusiastic couple. Their product range is excellent and their product knowledge is second to none. After an hour or so they had Raymond kitted out with a new helmet, boots, adventure jacket, hydro pack and heated gloves. I must say the heated gloves purchase was classic Raymond behaviour. Why would anyone with heated handlebar grips need heated gloves? Both Wilson and Raymond can be described as "cold rifted" which is Scottish for being sensitive to the cold. Alaska should be interesting!

From there we were off to Tiso Outdoor where he picked up a sleeping bag, liner, head torch, trousers and fleeces. He was now well kitted out for the trip. He came back to our house that night, had dinner with us and caught up on his mail, then set off back to his mother-in-law's laden with the goods that we had purchased earlier on his behalf, and also with those purchased that day. Christmas had come in January for Raymond!

We had agreed to meet up with all of the lads who had been on the May California trip. Pup (Raymond's younger brother) asked us to have it as a daytime session on Sunday the 25th of January. We readily agreed as he was travelling up from Bristol. In the end he had to call off due to personal circumstances. Sadly the Moose called off too, as his mother-in-law died the day before. I took the train into Glasgow, and bumped into Tree, who was on his way to meet Honda. We all headed to the Horsehoe Bar, where Hutch joined us. It was a good day with visits to a live music bar and a karaoke bar. Raymond surprised me when he wrote down a song and handed it to the host. To his horror, she enthusiastically invited him up to the floor to perform. "I thought it was for you to sing" he protested. Despite her valiant efforts she was never going to get him to perform.

Tree was very supportive of what we were doing and wished he was going too. We all encouraged him to get a motorcycle and come with us next time.

Next up was a visit to STV studios on the 29th of January; STV Glasgow had finally come good on their promise. We were welcomed by Nikki McCourt the producer and were directed to the canteen for a coffee. Wilson felt confident about the upcoming session but Raymond and I were decidedly nervous. My cousin John came down for a chat. John is a producer, and had managed to get our foot in the door of STV in the first place. We were also visited and prepped by Marelle Wilson, the production assistant. Marelle told us they had taken some video of Drena at Deafblind Scotland and had also used some of the footage I had sent in. I was glad it was all coming together at last. My apprehension was not helped when she told us there was only time for one take, no second chances. Finally we were led into the studio which was a very professional looking set-up. The presenter talked through her mike to the producers hidden behind smoked glass, while an assistant miked us up. The clock ticked down and before we knew it we were on. I made a nervous sounding start, but we all settled into it. They gave us nine minutes of airtime, which was way more than I expected. The end result looked good and we received a lot of positive feedback on our Facebook group site.

The next day I met up with my friend, Eddie Mitchell, for breakfast at Frankie and Benny's. Eddie worked alongside me at Digital for many years, and we have remained friends ongoing. Eddie took a redundancy package a year or so ago and was still in the process of looking for work. Our breakfast meetings had become an essential part of my non-working routine. I totally understood when he said he would miss them when I was gone. Eddie had also been very supportive of our fundraising. More supportive that he meant to be. He recently donated £50 for the second time. I called him and asked why he had made a second donation. It turned out he had forgotten he had donated already; he laughed it off and told me to keep it. Maybe he will donate again? On that Friday night we reached the £4000 mark, reaching my target amount for the departure point.

MotoFreight had sent through copies of our bikes Airway Bills. They were leaving that day heading for Toronto. Later that night I tracked the flight as it made its way across the Atlantic. "So far, so good", I thought.

Saturday the 31st of January started off with my by now common early awakening. I checked the status of the bikes. The flight they were booked on was on the runway at Toronto heading for Santiago, Chile. All looked as if it was going to plan. I visited my parents that day to allow me to say my goodbyes. Clearly they were thinking about the risks I would be facing and I was hoping with them both being in their eighties that nothing would happen to them while I was gone. Thankfully it all went well and everybody was able to handle the emotions. Not sure if that's the emotionally healthy answer but it worked for me.

I drove down to Galston later that night to pick up Raymond; we thought it would be easier if we travelled together the next morning to catch the early flight. We were both filled with excitement and apprehension about the journey ahead. Had anyone told us we would do this as seventeen-year-old bikers we would have thought they were mad.

"Unstoppable" From left to right Steve, Wilson and Raymond

The Trip Begins

Mon 2/3/15

As expected I had little sleep that night and was awake before the 3:45am alarm. We packed our things in Fat Boy (my Mini Countryman) and Amber drove us the 20 minutes or so to the airport. We said our goodbyes, ending with "See you in LA". I watched her drive off into the early morning darkness. Wilson arrived shortly after, and we moved smoothly through the check-in and security process. The flight was on time, and soon we were on our way to Amsterdam.

The transfer time was extremely tight so upon arrival we rushed through the expansive Schiphol airport in our heavy motorcycle jackets, racing towards our next flight. This time we were bound for São Paulo in Brazil, the long leg of the journey. Everything worked out fine, and we celebrated our on time arrival with a Brazilian beer. The final leg to Buenos Aires seemed to drag, a twelve-hour flight in total, and I was mightily glad to see the city appear below us. "We are finally here" I thought to myself as the gear was lowered for landing. We were all ready to arrive in Argentina at long last.

The driver was waiting for us as planned; a great start. We asked him to wait until we withdrew some cash, but the cash machine had other thoughts. Fortunately, he was willing to accept US dollars. After about thirty minutes we arrived at our Posada de las Aguilas Hotel and were grateful to be able to go straight to bed. I tossed and turned for a while unable to stop thinking, "this is it". I decided then that I would give myself the look of a real adventurer and grow a beard, a first for me. I fell asleep content in the knowledge I would save cash on shaving gel.

Tues 3/2/15

We had to rise sharply on Tuesday morning as we were meeting Sandra and Javier from Dakar Moto at 9am at the Petrobas fuel station near the airport entrance. Javier was a big burly guy who looked as if he might ride a Harley while Sandra looked like a typical Latin American lady, both looked to be in their fifties. They initially talked us through the process, sorted out insurance then took payment. Javier then headed off with the money while Sandra led us to the first of a few offices. She told us that Javier takes the money as she would be at risk of mugging on her public transport route home.

Initially it was all paperwork and payments but after a while we were allowed into the warehouse where our crated bikes awaited. It was hugely exciting to see them and even more exciting to watch them being unpacked. Thankfully they were all intact and looking great. Raymond was especially excited as this was his first sighting of Sheila. The whole process took most of the day, so it was late afternoon before we finally rode out of the customs area. Wilson and I needed fuel as our tanks had been over emptied and we all badly needed our tyres inflated. Unfortunately, none of us had brought a pump to the airport so we just had to ride them as they were on the short leg to the hotel. When we arrived back we decided to extend the hotel by another night. We felt that we would need the next day to fully prepare and check the bikes. This time we booked a triple room as single rooms were expensive.

Wed 4/2/15

We spent all day on the bikes. Mainly mounting bits to Raymond's such as bottle holders, fuel holders, a windscreen deflector and radiator guards. We sorted out tyre pressures and checked oil levels etc. I also helped Raymond organise huge amount of belongings with more thermals than an Arctic explorer and of all things, a shaving mirror.

That night we were meeting an Argentinean friend of a friend of Wilson's in downtown BA. Danny turned out to be in his sixties and a really nice guy. We enjoyed a great meal with him and we hoped to catch up with him again at his holiday home in Bariloche, Argentina. We asked Danny about the blue dollar which we had read about before leaving the UK. For some reason the Argentine Government constrain people from getting US dollars, so a whole black market has grown up around it. If you go to a bank or ATM you would receive at that time around 8 pesos to the dollar while a blue dollar exchange rate could be between 11 and 13. We badly needed blue dollars.

Argentina and Chile

Route Maps

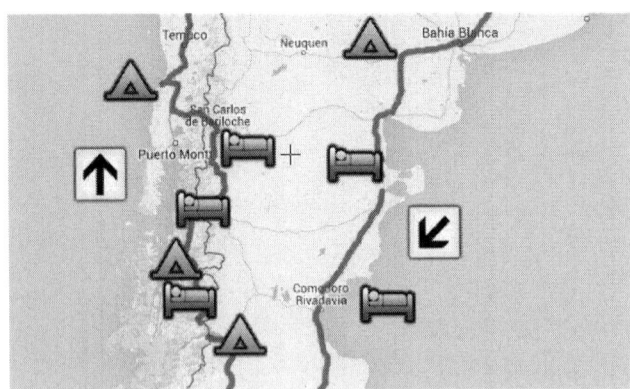

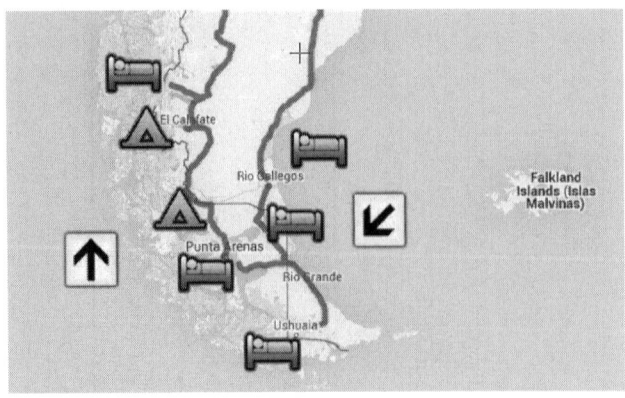

Thu 5/2/15

Sandra from Dakar Moto had recommended a great place to stay in Azul, Argentina, which was a reasonable distance for our first days riding. La Posta is run by a biker who had the nick name "Pollo" which translates into chicken. The ride out of Buenos Aires was fairly straightforward other than the fact that the first fuel station we came to would not take credit cards. We did eventually find a place, but not before we were all riding on fumes. We left the city, riding into the vast landscape that is Argentina. The countryside was very flat and fertile with long straight roads, a chance to make good progress. In fact, I was more concerned that we were making too much progress, with speeds of around 75mph. The roads were good and we had a long way to go to reach our starting point of Ushuaia.

When we finally reached Azul it looked to be a nice little town, and we searched for Pollo's place. After a bit of googling we got an address, enabling us to finally locate it. It was not at all the spacious rural campsite I had expected. It was a ramshackle bunch of buildings in the middle of town which looked locked up and closed for business. It was certainly full of character, with motorcycle logos painted everywhere on the walls. We walked around, convinced there was no one inside. I decided to give the door a good hard knock and was delighted when a guy in his 50s opened the door and welcomed us in. I initially thought he was Pollo, but in fact he was a friend of his. He advised us to pitch our tents in a small area of the yard next to a cracking John Lennon mural. He showed us the kitchen, workshop and some very basic toilet facilities. We loved it.

"Camp Pollo" a fantastic find

Pollo turned up and sure enough he was a friendly brawny little fella, filled with enthusiasm. Pollo's daughter, a translator by profession, came and translated for us. "He wants you to stay for a party tomorrow night" she told us. It sounded interesting, but we reluctantly told her that we had to press on. We asked her if she knew anyone who could trade dollars, and amazingly she said she had a work trip to London coming and she needed some. She gave us an initial $200 exchange to let us get to the supermarket. Pollo's friend from earlier walked Wilson and I to the supermarket, which was a few blocks away. It was a warm night and we were clearly in a poor to average part of town with people and dogs milling around everywhere. It felt very South American but not threatening at all. In fact, once he got us there he left us to shop with the locals. We bought some bread, cheese, ham and beer and decided we would eat in the kitchen area we had seen earlier. Raymond was particularly delighted with our choice and we all had a great night eating, drinking and looking at all of the traveller's notes and decorations on the walls of Pollo's place.

Fri 6/2/15

We slept well on our first night under canvas or whatever tents are made of nowadays. We left Pollo some dollars, a portable fire pit and a hat as our voluntary contribution since he didn't charge. A relative of Pollo's had also heard we were in the peso market so he showed up to make a trade for money.

We had decided the night before to head for a town called Rio Colorado as a target destination. Our route took us through a national park which offered more turns and gentle hills. Not long before reaching Rio Colorado we were hit by heavy rain, hailstones then blazing sun in rapid succession. "Just like Scotland minus the blazing sun", I thought. I also had to use my Rotopax fuel container just before we reached our destination due to the vast distances between fuel stations. They were very sturdy one gallon containers that were manufactured in the USA, and I was glad I had brought them.

When we finally reached Rio Colorado we fuelled up and asked the service station attendant if there was any good camping close by. He directed us to the municipal campsite a couple of miles further on. The site was large and cheap so we selected a river-side pitch and made camp. We checked out the toilets and showers which were in a word, disgusting. As we had no camping gas we needed to find something to eat, so we were pleased there was a little snack bar/café on-site. It did the job, providing pizza but the quality was really poor. That night I was surprised by the noise and music playing until around 1am in the campsite. It was something I was going to get used to.

Sat 7/2/15

We made a detour into the centre of the little town of Rio Colorado in search of camping gas. We had been directed to a camping shop which was run by an elderly couple with no English and no camping gas; still we all had fun trying to explain what we were after. It was baking hot so we

39

decided to stop off at a café for a drink and a snack. This was the first of our celebrity moments as a crowd gathered around us and the bikes. We enjoyed the friendly attention. Of course by now my beard had reached that short but cool look, not unlike George Clooney so I am sure that also had an impact.

We then made the long hot ride down to the resort town Puerto Mandryn. It was especially uncomfortable for me as my wrist and hands were being burned through gaps in my summer gloves. I ended up wrapping a bandage around my wrists as a temporary measure. The only other real incident of the journey was the loss of our Argentina map. Raymond and I saw it fly from Wilson's bike but it was too dangerous to stop. The good news was we had a spare.

Puerto Mandryn looked like a typical sea-side resort town as we made our way along the shore front to the campsite we had identified in advance. Just before that destination we were blocked by a marathon run. We talked to a few people, including the police, but bizarrely there was no way around. It was getting dark by the time we arrived, and we decided to look for a hotel. Fortunately the first hotel we tried worked out, as they had a triple room at a reasonable price. It was getting late by the time we unpacked the bikes and we ended up rushing out to find something to eat. Thankfully with this being Latin America, they were still serving at 11pm.

Sun 8/2/15

A guy who had been hanging around waiting for our camping spot as we packed up in Rio Colorado had warned us not to camp in any of the towns a day's drive south of Puerto Mandryn. He said "hotel ok but camping no" as he made the sign of a gun. With that firmly in mind we decided a hotel would be a good option, and rode south to the town of Coodoro Rivadavia, which was heavily industrial. We tried a big hotel in the centre but it was too expensive at around £30 each. Luckily they were friendly, and directed us to a cheaper option Hotel Elizabeth a few blocks away. It was clean, cheap, around £15 each, and had bike parking. That night we went in search of the blue dollar which was becoming the bane of our life in Argentina. We had been advised by the guy at reception to go to the casino, but they were offering a crazy rate. I guess this was just the front though, as a guy followed us from there, then approached us on a street corner offering cambio (exchange). We felt a bit exposed on the street with the memory of the gun sign in our heads, and as he was only offering 11 pesos to the dollar we declined.

Mon 9/2/15

Next morning we decided we would head for a place 100 miles or so above Rio Gallegos which was the last city before Ushuaia. The ride down was long and for the first time we experienced the fierce Patagonian winds. We had been warned via books and fellow travellers of how bad they were, but as with everything, you have to experience it for yourself. They are ferocious, and can last throughout a journey of over 100 miles. You have to lean into the wind hoping there will be no sudden change of direction. You sometimes hit little lulls, which are scary, as you have no idea which direction it's going to come from next. The very worst part is when you have the combination of a bus coming towards you and the wind hitting the side of you. There is a real shock wave after the bus passes by. Passing a bus or a truck in the wind is equally terrifying. The trick in both cases is to accelerate which goes against your natural instinct. The other experience of the ride was the herds of Lama's roaming freely by the side of the road. There were hundreds of them. Big beautiful beasts, but not something you want to hit on a motorbike.

When we reached our planned destination we found it was grubby and accommodation-less. We pressed on to Rio Galles and found the Hotel Comercio, which fitted our needs. This was our first 400 plus miles day of the trip.

Tues 10/2/15

Rio Gallegos had always been the planned final staging post for our journey to Tierra del Fuego. It was close enough to the Chilean border and the ferry port to allow time for any delays. It was a modern town and seemed to be fairly prosperous. I was pleased we had inadvertently reached there the night before, due to the lack of accommodation further north. We had breakfast and packed up the bikes in what was a chilly but bright morning and set off for the Chilean border.

The ride out of town was amusing (for me) as a pack of dogs first of all chased Raymond then proceeded to chase Wilson in an interested, but definitely non-aggressive way. Not far out of town we started to see bikers heading in the same direction, all of us battling against the fierce winds. After about half an hour we came to our first overland border crossing. I had read that this was one of the easiest crossings and hoped it would be the case. After stopping at the first building we were ushered on a half mile or so further up the road. The place was jam packed, so we got into line. We noticed other people filling in forms, so we dispatched Raymond to get us some. It was a long hot and slow process but after a couple of hours we were on our way in Chile.

The ride to the port of Manantiales was around a further 20 minutes, and just as we approached, traffic came streaming towards us. A good omen I thought, as there was probably a ferry just unloading. We arrived at the back of what must have been a mile-long queue of trucks, buses and cars. We pushed on past up to the dockside where another bike was waiting; the ferry was in and they were starting to load it. It all looked pretty dodgy, the sea was rough, and there was no actual harbor, just a concrete ramp with the ferry hovering by using its engines to keep it there. Apparently they decided to stop the loading process when a guy in a pickup truck pushed his way past. His truck nearly toppled into the sea when the ferry pulled off just as he hit the ramp. He was very lucky indeed. There was no ticket office or information, but we were told by a Spanish speaking Swiss lady biker who had arrived with her husband, that the service was suspended until maybe around 6pm when the winds died down. There was nothing for it but to go into the café for some food and coffee. After our food the tiredness caught up with all three of us, and we all fell asleep with our heads on the table. When we woke up Wilson and I went outside with the bikes, while Raymond chatted to a German biker couple who gave him lots of useful info on Chile.

Finally the ferry service resumed, and we were ushered aboard. The crossing cost about £10 and took about half an hour. The bikes were not tied down, so we stayed with them. We had finally made it to the territory of Tierra del Fuego (Land of Fire). The landscape at this point was similar to the mainland, both flat and vast. We spotted the sign for a town called Cerro Sombrero which appealed to us. We rode the ten miles or so, then pulled into this small remote town.

We fueled up first; it seemed much more expensive than Argentina but I am sure we were being ripped off as we had no Chilean pesos and were paying in Argentinian pesos. Then we stopped off outside a hotel to check the maps and decided we would ride further that night. However as we rode out of town we noticed the German and Swiss biker couples pulled over by what looked like a community centre. We stopped to talk and discovered there was a shop and that they planned to stay at a hostel in town. We looked at our watches and as it was 8pm, agreed to do the same.

The hostel was a ramshackle single storied building, pretty basic, but clean. We all loved its quirkiness with a paw waving mechanical cat and a picture of Santa Claus inside. We sat in the communal area that evening and chatted to the other bikers over dinner. Karin and Markus from Switzerland were nearing the end of a world tour while Silvia and Heiko from Germany were extensively touring South America.

"The Cerro Sombrero Hostel"

Wed 11/2/15

I woke up on Wednesday to a bright and sunny morning after a good night's rest. Thankfully the wind had calmed down as we were approaching our first gravel roads, known locally as ripeo. The host served us bread, cheese and ham with tea before departing. The gravel road ran alongside a brand new road that was close to completion, so it was a little frustrating that we were having to slip and slide on the ripeo road, alongside this fresh inviting tarmac. After a good twenty miles or so Wilson suggested we just use the tarmac road. I was initially reluctant, but was so relieved to be on a smooth surface again. Before long the official road turned to tarmac, relaxing us briefly before it turned back to ripeo.

Our destination of Ushuaia was in the Argentinian part of Tierra del Fuego, so we had another border ahead. The crossing back into Argentina was quiet and straight forward, although we had a small scare over the fact that everyone else seemed to be carrying the very important form Sandra at Dakar had told us about. Ours had been taken by the authorities in the mainlandd, but in the end we discovered the 'very important form' is issued again on entry. As we left I noticed a little hostel in San Sebastian at the border which was to come in useful later on.

The gravel turned to tarmac on the Argentinian side, and we made good progress to our next fuel and coffee stop at the islands largest town, Rio Grande.

Petrol is always pumped for you, and this time it was by an efficient young man in his twenties with a beanie hat and bandana to keep out the chill. I wondered what it would be like to do that job at the bottom of the world. The ride down to Ushuaia became more interesting by the mile. Mountains loomed in the distance signaling our destination. Open plains turned to rolling countryside then became coastal just before the long steep climb over the mountain passes. It was raining now so we were all wearing bright yellow rain suits.

On the way we had stopped to secure our luggage by the roadside. Raymond let out a yell as Sheila tipped over into the soft gravel, it took all of us to lift her back up, but no damage done.

It was with a great feeling of satisfaction that we finally arrived in Ushuaia, after all those months, actually years, of planning. The town itself was set on a bay, with a cold rainy wind blowing in. We filled up our tanks and headed to a hostel called La Posta, which had been used and recommended by some predecessors. The girl in reception was French, and friendly but sadly there was no availability. She recommended an unofficial hostel nearby which she described as excellent. We were glad to take up her advice.

The unofficial hostel was located right in the centre of town amongst the tourist shops serving the Antarctica bound cruise ships. It was chaotic with ramshackle buildings and tents pitched closely together in the garden, but looked as though it would work. A bonus was the owner was happy to exchange US dollars at a decent rate. After signing in we were shown to a Porta cabin with six bunks in it, and the door hanging off. Two of the bunks were clearly occupied. We all looked at each other shaking our head thinking this would not do. We went back and told the guy we were looking for a private shared room, to which he said "no problem" and asked us to wait. Soon after decanting some tired looking youths, he showed us a comfortable room with two sets of bunk beds. We went through our normal unpacking process, which always included getting electronics charged. Raymond proved to be very quick on the draw with the charger pistol.

We headed off into town and stumbled on a restaurant that looked good although I was a little concerned about the price but was too tired and hungry to argue. I think this was my first conscious concern that we were sometimes eating holiday style rather than adventure style. In the end we had a delicious Argentinian steak (Lomo) and chips (Papas Frites). Then it was back to the hostel for a good sleep. The scary thing was I was last in the queue for the bed allocation so I was relegated to the top bed which was quite a height with no safety barrier. It took me a little time to settle into the idea that I must not attempt to step out of bed in the middle of the night.

Thu 12/2/15

Thursday morning was sunshine and showers. This was a major point in our journey; today for the first time we were heading north. There had been a discussion the night before around our next steps and since the ferry across to Punta Arenas only sailed once a day at 2pm, we felt that we should move further north to make sure we caught it. It was a sensible decision but I still felt disappointed as I would have liked a couple more days in Ushuaia.

We breakfasted at the Banana Café, run by a very friendly young Argentinian with great English. We then packed up and headed out to take a photo of us beside the Ushuaia sign. When we pulled up there was a bunch of Argentinian bikers already parked up. We had an interesting exchange in pigeon English and Spanish. Bikers united no matter what language! The ride out of Ushuaia was fantastic with amazing views of the snow-capped mountains. It's incredible how you can get a completely different perspective by riding in the opposite direction. We had a short distance of just over a hundred miles to get to our planned destination of Rio Grande which would be our staging post for the ferry. For the first time I felt as if we were not in a rush and we pulled over at a great view point on the Paso Garibaldi (Garibaldi Pass). A pretty looking woman who was there with her husband ran over immediately to take photos of us. She was warm and smiley and gave us all a kiss before setting off.

"Ushuaia" the southernmost city

We finally arrived at Rio Grande and stopped at the same petrol station as we had used on the way in. The same young man was pumping fuel, efficient as ever. We checked out accommodation options on the Sat navs and found a campsite close by, or at least it used to be; there was nothing there on arrival. We then checked for hotels and found one downtown. Riding through the town was unpleasant with aggressive drivers and a lot of run down streets. We were getting a bit jaded, then the hotel guy told us there was no availability. We tried across the road at a Casino hotel, but that had no off-street parking for the bikes. By this time we had had our fill of Rio Grande, and decided to get the hell out of Dodge!

I had noticed a small Hostel next to the Chilean border in San Sebastian, on the way south. We hoped they would have rooms available. The ride turned from relaxed to tense as the winds were increasingly fierce as we made our way along the coast. We stopped at what looked like a hostel on the Argentinian side of the border, it was actually a restaurant and shop, where we took the opportunity to stock up on supplies. The border crossing was quiet and easy at that time of night. The ride from the Argentine exit to the Chilean entry was horrible, due to the ripeo and the setting sun in our eyes.

We cleared into Chile and rode the few hundred yards to the hostel. Wilson checked it out and we were delighted to learn that they had space. The Hostel was excellent based on our new standards; available, fairly clean with cold running water. Our hosts were an older Chilean lady and her husband I presumed, and a younger Venezuelan girl. We had lots of laughs as we struggled to communicate with each other. We drank the beer we had bought at the shop earlier, then had a basic but filling meal in the hostel restaurant.

Fri 13/2/15

The hostel lady confirmed that the road to Porvenir was ripeo all the way. Eighty miles of ripeo was a challenging and daunting prospect. I nearly lost

48

Boris in the first half mile after drifting over the thicker stuff while checking my sat nav. From there on in it was full concentration all the way. I kept repeating Clive of Motoscotland's words "trust the bike, look ahead of you". Then our journey was interrupted by the largest herd of sheep I had ever seen blocking the road. It was an amazing sight, nothing but sheep to the end of the horizon. We watched in awe as a local simply drove through them, cutting a path as he went. We geared up and followed the next passing car, doing the same thing. It was a brilliant experience, especially when we reached the end of the flock and found a Gaucho with a horse and a pack of excited dogs. After a fairly tense ride, which included a rock being spat up from my wheel onto my big toe (ouch), we finally pulled into the port of Porvenir where the ferry was docked.

"A Sheep block in Chile"

Inside the ferry building we joined the queue for tickets. We had ordered them the night before but had received no confirmation, nor had made any payment. We hoped the ferry operator took credit cards as we had no Chilean pesos. A kind Chilean guy who spoke English checked for us, and of course the answer was no. Luckily they did take Argentinian pesos, so we were fine. I still have no idea if our pre-booking had any impact, but I suspect not.

We boarded the ferry and quickly found a spot inside. It was a much bigger ferry than the last one. We joined the queue for coffee, but could not understand the system. Finally we worked out that we needed to get a ticket, then pay a guy to get another ticket, then finally when our number came up we would be served. In the end we gave up for a while; it was far too busy and hot. Later on I heard our number being called, and got our hot coffee, supplemented with sandwiches bought the night before. During all of this the ship had not left dock. Next came an announcement that the ship had a technical issue, and that they were working on. This was translated for us by a young Chilean who lived in Porvenir but was studying mechanical engineering in Punta Arenas. He showed us pictures of him leaping through the air in a quad bike. Apparently he was regional champion.

After about an hour's delay the ferry finally departed. We took a look outside and realized it was much more comfortable to be in the sunshine. Almost as soon as we were out there we spotted dolphins swimming alongside the ship. It was amazing to watch them frolicking around. We then had a long conversation with a sixty-year-old Aussie guy who was there with five of his mates on a fishing trip. He was an interesting guy who had made his money from a flour grinding business, and planned to spend it buying a yacht and sail around the Mediterranean for the next ten years. Sounded like a brave but inspiring plan. He was equally impressed with our trip. After a relaxing two hours of sailing, the ship pulled into Puerto Arenas.

We had had a recommendation for the Hostel Patagonia from the Australian which, after an unsuccessful trip to the cash machine, we set off to look for it. The only similar name that came up in our sat nav was the Hotel Patagonia Bed and Breakfast so we tried that. Unfortunately after a lot of circling we could not see it either. We tried another random hostel, but they had no bike parking. We then went for a cruise along the sea front, and spotted what looked like a fairly expensive hotel. We were getting tired and decided to check it out. In the end it worked out at $56 each, with parking and breakfast included, so we agreed to go for it. It was a typically nice 'Holiday Inn' style hotel with a spacious room, modern bathroom and a sea view. We even had the use of a pool and a sauna which along with the buffet breakfast in the morning, we took full advantage. The hotel was busy with runners who were doing 7 marathons in 7 continents in 7 days. Very impressive although as yesterday's final marathon in Antarctica had been canceled due to bad weather it would at least be 8 days. We had a simple dinner that night; pizza and beer which was delicious.

Sat 14/2/15

Celebrating Valentine's Day was my priority when I woke up from a good sleep. I checked my mail and found a greeting from Amber. I sent her a message, and soon after she sent back a photo of the roses I had ordered with the title "the boy done good"! I managed to get her on FaceTime for a short conversation which went well. By now I was really glad we had arranged a reunion in LA.

The road shadowed the coast for a while then cut inland across vast plains. Towards the end of the 130 mile ride the area became much hillier and finally the impressive snow-capped peaks of the Andes loomed in front of us. This was a real milestone for me as I love the power and grandeur of mountains.

Puerto Natales was a nice little town set on a vast lake surrounded by mountains clearly catering for tourists. We pulled up at the tourist information office and went inside to check out our camping options. The young girl inside spoke good English directing us to her favorite campsite in town. The place was a combination of hostel, campsite and restaurant.

It had little fenced in sheltered areas for each pitch to combat the Patagonian winds which was very useful. At a price of 5000 Chilean pesos, around £5, it was just what we needed.

"Patagonian graffiti in Puerto Natales"

That evening we walked into town to a pub restaurant recommended by a local camping shop. We enjoyed their special dish, Papas Frites with chicken and cheese. This was washed down with some tasty local ale. Our evening was severely disturbed until around 4am by a live band playing local music right next door. When the band stopped the dogs started barking, maybe looking for an encore.

Sun 15/2/15

Despite the noise disturbance I felt as if I had had a decent sleep. I was glad we had managed to purchase gas for our stoves the previous evening and I had some coffee sachets left over from the hotel in Puerto Arenas. It was great to just sit there with my coffee before the others finally awoke. Then we wandered into town and found a good coffee and breakfast stop on the shore front. They also had free Wi-Fi which worked for the others but sadly not for me, for reasons unknown. Next we did our first shop of the trip at the local supermarket. It was important to me that we were moving into a camping and cooking phase otherwise the trip budget would quickly run out of control. We had decided that morning to stay put for another night to allow ourselves a rest day. It was great just to chill and catch up on the laundry. We wandered about a mostly closed down town that night, but ultimately ended up in a bar. We sat next to a couple of Aussies, Dwaine and Jerry, and discovered that they too were on a motorcycle adventure. We enjoyed their company and swapped contact details hoping we might hook up further north. It was on that night there was the first open squabble amongst us, the three amigos. It was never going to be easy putting three guys together 24x7.

Mon 16/2/15

I was up before the others and rustled up some coffee with eggs and bread. I was packing up by the time Wilson stirred. I had decided to head down to the internet cafe on the shore front and chill while the other two got themselves together. Raymond was last to rise and I think felt a bit left behind. We all agreed we would set a target for departure in future so everyone knew the schedule. The proper coffee, toast and jam was great and I was able to catch up on my email etc. Wilson joined me in a while and soon after that Raymond. "I have a warning light on my bike" he said, looking concerned. We pulled out Wilson's user manual and identified it as an engine issue; the bike had gone into an emergency ride with care mode. I googled BMW dealers while Wilson made contact with the BMW technician Stevie Cowan at Douglas Park. Stevie was able to show Wilson what to check via FaceTime. Just superb to see how technology can work in a situation like this. Wilson did the check and tightened the screws as advised. Soon after that the warning light disappeared. We were pretty sure it had corrected itself, but we will never know for sure.

We then set off for our next destination, Torres Del Paine National Park. I was looking forward to this bit as this was one of the mountain ranges with dramatically shaped peaks. We rode up to Cerro Castillo where we had a coffee in an overpriced tourist trap, then headed to the park, initially on tarmac but ultimately on ripeo again. My experience was that the ripeo started bad, with no defined wheel track but settled down after a while. We finally got closer to the mountain range and were in awe of their grandeur. We had been advised by the Aussies to camp at the base of a lake looking onto the mountains. Their recommendation was spot on, as we had a dream camping pitch with good clean facilities. I had picked up a brochure which pictured the mountain range, naming the peaks. I lay inside my tent holding the brochure up and realized I has exactly the same view, and what a view it was.

"A room with a view"

Tues 17/2/15

It rained pretty hard during the night but had stopped by the time I got up. I enjoyed pottering around in such a stunning setting until the rain came back with a vengeance and we were forced to pack up in the wet. This was made more bearable by the fact we had a shelter to take refuge under. I found the ripeo a little easier to deal with in the wet on the return leg back to Cerro Castillo. By the time we got there the sun was out and it was hot.

We chose a local little café for breakfast and coffee rather than the tourist trap and it was a wise choice. We were now well used to the South America coffee routine, where you are served a mug of hot water and a jar of Nescafé is placed on the table for you to spoon it in.

After that we smoothly exited Chile and bumped into Argentina, thanks to a nasty official making us fill in Spanish only forms for our bikes. Luckily there were some helpful English speaking natives to assist. It was interesting that the border crossing process, despite being between the same countries, was never the same. We chatted to a girl in the queue from Switzerland. Her name was Simone and she had teamed up with Dwaine and Jerry whom we had met in Puerto Natales, and was planning to meet them again later that day.

The ride up to El Calafate finally had us on the famous Ruta 40 that stretches north up through Argentina. In the past it was mainly ripeo but it's now mostly paved. It was once again Montana style scenery with huge sky's and endless vistas. We hit the fiercest winds of the trip in the final approach to town making it a very uncomfortable ride for a half hour or so. I did not enjoy the weight of my bike in the ripeo but was thankful for it in the winds.

We rode into town and stumbled upon a great looking campsite with a 'jobs worth' kind of security guard, who kept us waiting at the gate until reception was clear. Check in was very professional and we were allocated a pole with a number on it to put next to the tent. I was expecting we would have a nice pitch each. We were told to cross the river at the second bridge and pick a spot. It was mayhem with tents pitched everywhere. As we looked for a corner we spotted Dwaine and Jerry, and also Simone, the Swiss girl we had talked to at the border. We all squeezed into a minuscule spot and set up camp.

I was ready first so went to talk to the Aussie boys where I was greeted with a warm welcome, and a cold beer. Wilson and Raymond joined us shortly after and a good night was had by all. The reason the campsite was in mayhem was due to a music festival that going on. The music was blaring loudly all over the campsite as I bedded down for the night, inches from my neighbors in all directions.

Wed 18/2/2015

The noise never abated at all during the night, and a very determined group were still partying at six in the morning when I decided to get up. As I left the tent I saw a group of young Argentinian boys and girls gathered around a fire pit with a ghetto blaster blasting out. I made my way across a small wooden bridge to the toilets. These were expansive, and had just been recently cleaned, which was a result. After cleaning up I headed back to the tent to brew some coffee. As I approached my tent one of the young party animals came over and asked me to join them.

"We have Argentine whisky" he gleefully told me.

I politely declined.

The rest of the campsite started to stir including our new found Australian mates, and the packing up process commenced. I had a picture taken with the party animals, and something about them reminded me of the images I had seen of young Argentinian boys captured in the Falklands war. I remember how young and scared they looked.

"The party animals and me"

We departed from the campsite around 10:30am (after waiting for Raymond) and immediately joined a long queue for petrol. We had talked about just heading north, but I felt as if we needed a review of our plans so I called a meeting. Danny the guy we met in Buenos Aires had invited us to stay with him and his wife further north in Bariloche. We all wanted to do it, but I was beginning to feel it was putting us under too much pressure and that we might miss some really good stuff on the way. We all agreed reaching Danny's wasn't realistic for the time when he would be around, so decided to slow down. We picked a destination of El Chalten located at the foot of Mount Fitzroy.

I think everyone felt good about the decision as we rode out of town. Getting there involved retracing our steps for 20 miles or so to rejoin Ruta 40. From there it was then a fairly short ride north, then a diversion to the east.

El Chalten was a scenic mountain town not unlike you might see in the US, Canada or even Austria. We stopped at the tourist information centre located in the bus station on the edge of town. Wilson knocked his pannier into mine as he pulled up jolting me forward. He was concerned but I laughed it off remembering how many years ago my Belgian friend Kurt had responded to me doing the same to him.

"It's just a tin box, made for bumps".

The temperature was quite low in the mountains so we opted for a hostel. We were given a few options of which the first was full; the second worked out fine. Next we took a walk along the Main Street and dined on a tasty pizza, then called in at a German Brew pub for a couple of quality cold ales.

Thu 19/2/15

Next morning we had an early start, as we wanted to make up a good few miles. We had to retrace our steps to Ruta 40, then head north. Ruta 40 was fantastic with its never ending landscape and a mixture of sweeping bends and huge straights. That was until we hit the ripeo. Initially it was just the usual scary and unpredictable kind, but after around twenty miles we hit a section that was sticky wet clay. We were all brought to a sliding halt. There was a new unsurfaced road being built alongside the clay pit so Wilson decided to try that. Unfortunately it was worse and we had to push him out of there. There was nothing for it but to proceed with caution. I found the non-tire tracks which is normally the slippy bit was best. In effect the slippy became the grippy. Fortunately it only lasted for another mile or so, before returning to gravel. Gravel now felt incredibly easy in relative terms. The ripeo lasted for 80 kilometers in total before tarmac and normal service would resume. On the final section of ripeo Raymond and I were progressing cautiously, standing on the pegs of our big adventure bikes when a wee guy sitting on a typical small road bike swiftly rode past us just as if we were standing still; he waved cheerfully. We both burst out laughing at our utter humiliation.

"Wilson on Ruta 40"

We pressed on northwards, eventually stopping for petrol and coffee, where we met a bunch of Argentinian bikers, similar to us in age, on a 'boy's trip'. They were very impressed by our trip and waved to us when we bumped into them several times thereafter on the road. We finally pulled into our destination of Perito Moreno after just over 400 miles of riding. It had a long main street not unlike a traditional American town. We were just checking out a hostel from the outside when an old guy with a braided pony tail ushered us over to the other side of the road. He had set up a mini campsite in his garden which was perfect, with basic but clean toilet facilities and flat ground. We quickly pitched up our tents for the night and walked into the little town centre to buy some bread and powdered soup for a 'stay in' night. There was only one other tent on-site and it turned out to be the perfect relaxation and star gazing opportunity.

Fri 20/2/15

The ride the next day would take us back into Chile, and on to the famous Caraterra Austral. This road was reputed to be one of the best motorcycling roads on the planet. We set off that morning blindly following the sat nav, crossing back into Chile on the way. This time they made us put our luggage through a scanner, a complete pain when you're on a motorcycle. We had gone quite a distance when Raymond informed us through the intercom that his sat nav was displaying 'ferry'. We had in fact taken a great road, but the wrong one, and we rolled into a little lakeside town with a great name, Chile Chico.

We pulled up at the dock and went to check on the ferry. The good news was that there was one later that day; the bad news was they had no space. We questioned, pleaded and cajoled and finally we were told by the very unhelpful assistant that we could go. Unfortunately that was not the case for the people behind us, including a couple of backpackers on foot who were told they needed to wait until the next day. We spotted them later that afternoon chilling with a glass of wine in the sun. That's exactly the attitude you need in South America.

The ferry crossing over General Carrera Lake was very scenic, with impressive Mountains in all directions. The ferry dropped us off at a town called Puerto Ibanez, which was the start for us of the Caraterra Austral. It did not disappoint, with its endless climbs, dips and curves and there were a lot more scenic views to come. We had targeted the town of Colhaique that night and after several attempts we found a little apartment hotel which did the trick. It had two rooms and as luck would have it, it was my turn for my own room. Raymond was to discover that night that he had lost his wallet. We were all carrying a mugger's wallet with less cash and cards, but still it was a blow for him. We did a bit of back tracking to the fuel station etc. but to no avail.

Sat 21/2/15

I had a good sleep in my own little room, enjoying my space, which by now was a luxury item for us all. Breakfast was served by some friendly women, in a separate building close to our apartment. After that we all just lazed around making the most of the good Wi-Fi and the comfort of the place. I finally managed to catch up with Amber who was visiting my parents that day.

Later on we visited the supermarket for supplies and also purchased a bucket, sponge and shampoo to clean the bikes. We had spied a hose in the hotel car park, and thought this would be an ideal opportunity to wash the grime off the bikes and change the air filters. It was a messy but a necessary job. The town itself was mid-sized and had a main street full of shops and restaurants. Wilson and I bought Raymond a replacement wallet in a market stall which we planned to give him on his up and coming birthday.

Sun 22/2/15

We checked out of the apartment and re-joined the Caraterra Austral. The road continued to fully live up to its reputation, with amazing scenery and fantastic twisties. We had been warned that the road would close ahead at 1pm through to 5pm while roadworks were carried out, but we were fairly confident that we would be through it on time. After many sumptuous tarmac miles we came across our first Austral ripeo. Unfortunately it coincided with a twisty mountain pass, making it even more challenging. We were not long into it when Raymond stalled on a sharp bend and lost his balance, and Sheila.

I was riding behind and stopped to help him lift her up. Luckily there was no damage to rider or bike. Naturally enough it spooked him a bit but we moved on uphill. At one point I glanced up and saw an amazing glacier; t was only for a few seconds but amazing just the same. I checked with the others but they had missed it, as I nearly had, due to concentrating on the road. We continued down the other side of the pass feeling confident that we were well past the road closure point when we came to a road closed barrier. It was 1:15pm and we had missed the cut-off.

We insisted, cajoled and pleaded with the tiny Chilean lady on point but she was having none of it. She was five feet but as Wilson said "the most powerful woman in Chile". There was nothing for it but to relax. We got out our camping chairs and stoves and cooked soup in the middle of the Caraterra Austral, which must be fairly unique. We had visitors from the line of traffic behind including a couple of real estate agent ladies from Santiago. Their parting message was "you must try the lamb".

"Chilling on the Chilean Caraterra Austral"

The road opened at 5pm as scheduled and we were once again on our way into terrible roads which had been ripped up by roadworks. A few miles on Raymond had his second fall, this time a bit harder, and scarier but again no harm done. A few passing car drivers and I made sure he was alright, and once again we were on our way. The difference in confidence in off road riding between Wilson and Raymond and I was quite marked. Wilson was mainly riding a few miles in front relaxed and enjoying himself, while Raymond and I comforted and reassured each other through the process. I was glad I had that support as I would have felt very alone and demoralised without it. We were both very relieved that night when we arrived at our destination.

Puyuhuapi was a small village set at the head of a lake surrounded by mountains. We quickly found the campsite and checked in. We were placed in a cow shed type building where there were three tents already pitched. I have never seen six tents so tightly squashed into such a small space. In retrospect we should have moved on as it was way too crushed. Wilson had a night from hell bordered by Raymond's incredibly squeaky camp bed and my snoring. Unusually, but understandably, he was first up.

Mon 23/2/15

Next morning we discovered we still had roadworks to negotiate; fortunately we managed without incident. It was Raymond's birthday that day, so he had free reign to stop and take photos as he pleased. We would normally be complaining due to the lack of progress and the heat: he really took advantage of this with frequent stops in the sun. He picked a great day for it as the scenery was once again amazing. We stopped on a bridge watching several rafter's battle through the most amazing aquamarine coloured fast flowing river.

At one point a 4x4 passed me and the driver waved me down. He turned out to be a guy we had chatted to at the road block the day before.

"There's something hanging from the back of your bike" he said.

It turned out to be my mudguard, which had given up after a bolt had sheared off on the punishing roads. I removed the one remaining fixing, and stuffed it under one of my luggage straps.

The gravel finally ended at a place called Futaleufu which was set in a valley with a 360 degrees' view of the mountains. It had a park in the town square and lots of café's, supermarkets and shops. We parked up and wandered around in the heat, desperate for coffee. Unfortunately it was 5pm, and for some reason they were all closed. We grabbed some snacks from the supermarket, then went back to the bikes for a pow-wow. Our original destination had been Esquel in Argentina but that was still two hours away and included a border crossing. We all agreed we should stay put and celebrate Raymond's birthday.

As per the newly decided birthday rules Raymond got to choose the accommodation, and he went for the Patagonian Hostel recommended by the young Tourist Information officer and his disinterested young female side-kick. The Hostel was excellent and as a birthday bonus Raymond had his own room. We had a good dinner that evening savoring the Chilean Lamb that had been recommended to us by the two women while we were stuck at the road closure the previous day. We presented Raymond with his new wallet and as a special treat the Argentinian family at the next table sang happy birthday in Spanish. I'm sure it's one he will always remember.

Tues 24/02/15

I managed to FaceTime Amber in the morning and ensure all was well back home. I always got uneasy after several days out of contact. I also talked to my friend Eddie who had shown a massive amount of interest and enthusiasm for the trip.

The sun was shining and I was feeling good. We decided we would make some good progress this morning all of the way to Bariloche the place where we had hoped to meet Danny. This would mean a long day in the saddle. I had put Boris on his centre stand to do some nuts and bolts checks after all the rough roads. Despite having warned Raymond the previous day not to take the fully loaded bike off the centre stand on his own, I did exactly that and Boris fell on his side, much to the amusement of two hostel worker girls who were outside having a smoke. The fall was on grass, with no harm done and we all had a good laugh at my predicament.

Then we set off for the border, which was about 10 kilometres up the road. Once through that I decided I would do some Go-Pro filming on the ripeo. I pulled over to adjust my camera putting Boris onto his side stand. I felt the ground was a bit soft but did not expect him to topple over; unfortunately he did. He had landed in the ditch and it took the three of us to get him upright. No real harm done other than some scratches on the pannier stickers, and a loose wing mirror. Very annoying though. We exited the ripeo at a town called Trevelin, stopping for coffee and a burger. 100 miles further on I discovered I had left my wallet there. It was my mugger's wallet, so not a lot of cash and a travel card I could easily cancel. Still it was very irritating, made even more so by the trouble I had cancelling the Travel Cash card.

We were fairly close to Bariloche when Raymond let out a yell over the intercom.

"I've been stung" he yelped.

We all pulled over and he quickly removed his glove revealing several wasp stings on his hand. My first aid kit was the most accessible so I handed him my sting and bite cream. Not long after he applied it the pain receded, although he noticed his skin was peeling. We agreed this was effective but potent stuff.

We arrived that night in Bariloche around 8pm with some vague instructions from Danny on how to find a particular hostel. It was dark by the time we did find his hostel which turned out to be now converted into long let serviced apartments. I was glad, as it looked too expensive anyway. We went on to a little hotel I had spotted during the search, and agreed a rate which was more than I wanted to pay, but it was after 10pm and desperation was setting in.

We unloaded the luggage and made several treks to and from the room. The male owner was particularly unfriendly and stand offish with us. The final straw was when he insisted we move the bikes to another area for no logical reason. Enough was enough, we said we were moving despite the hassle of repacking the bikes. We tried another hostel down the road where the owner said he was full, but took the time to direct us elsewhere. On our way Wilson was approached by a couple at a junction who said they had a hostel. It was dark, in fact there had just been a power cut in the town, and we had no idea if they were genuine. So what did we do? We followed them into the darkness. We ended up down a dirt road where they showed us the place by smartphone torchlight. Hostel Los Maitenes turned out to be an excellent find, in fact so good we stayed there for two days.

Wed 25/2/15

Day two in Bariloche was relaxing as we did the tourist thing, wandering around downtown. It's a tourist town next to a beautiful lake, and surrounded by mountains. We traded dollars for a compromise blue rate of $11.95 to the peso. It was there we discovered they would give a better exchange for big notes i.e. $50 or $100 rather than the $20's Wilson and I were carrying. Still no idea why. I would have imagined it would have been the opposite.

We searched for bulbs for my spot light which had popped somewhere along the way. I managed to get what I thought was the correct bulb but it did not fit. I discovered when I got home that that particular bulb comes complete with a snap-in fitment. I am sure had I known they would have been readily available. I will know in future.

"Lago Nahuel Huapi - Bariloche"

We spent a quiet night at the hostel rustling up some bland food, but as luck would have it the owner of the hostel was barbecuing that evening, and was kind enough to hand us some delicious steak, which we thoroughly enjoyed.

Thu 26/2/15

We left Bariloche to make our first crossing of the famous Andes mountain range. Just like the Rockies, Alps or Himalayas the very name exudes power and magnitude; I love mountains. The crossing was fairly low level for the Andes although we reached around 9000 feet which is nearly two times the height of Ben Nevis. There was pretty green countryside, with long gentle assents and descents on good paved roads. We left Argentina and headed towards the Chilean entry post but after about 12 kilometres there was still no sign of the familiar collection of border crossing buildings. We stopped to discuss this as they had previously been a few kilometres apart or less, so this seemed odd. We agreed we should turn around and thankfully decided to stop and ask a backpacker. It was in fact further on down the road, probably 20 kilometres or more. Another lesson learned on the variations of border crossings.

After entering Chile, we stopped at a local café for lunch where there was no formal menu, just some rambling words from a shy boy in his early teens. The resulting chicken and chips was excellent. A couple of backpackers tried to serenade us for money, but it was not for us as we were on a budget too. I saw my first example of what looked to be a severely under fed South American dog outside, so I gave him a breakfast bar I was carrying as a snack.

We finally joined Chile Ruta 5 which is part of the official Pan American highway. It was like the M25 motorway but with combine harvesters, mothers and children crossing the road, and food stalls on the hard shoulder. The speed limit was 120 kph and most people were doing at least that. Scary, but you somehow got used to it. The countryside was stark and industrial. Probably the worst bit of the trip to date.

We arrived at our chosen destination of Valdivia which is famous for German Beer breweries. The town looked unattractive and I was hot and suffering from a searing headache. I had been having pains down my face since our lunch stop and was feeling a bit concerned about it. We pulled into a fuel station to get our bearings. When I removed my helmet I discovered a small seed the size of an apple pip was stuck in the lining at my temple area. Simply removing the seed solved the headache, that was a relief.

We stumbled across a hostel where some Argentinian bikers were parked. Raymond and I took a look around the hostel, but it was hot and looked grubby and we were keen to camp that night. A guy in the street with a little English directed us to a place 10 kilometres south of town where we found a little riverside campsite. The route into it was a scary steep off road descent, with a corner by the edge of the river but we managed to get round there just fine. The site layout was cramped in Scottish terms but spacious in Chilean, with at least a couple of feet between tents. It worked well for that night. We dined in a local café, now feeling a bit fed up with each other's company.

Fri 27/2/15

We left the campsite in good time heading back into Valdivia for breakfast in the square. The place looked nice that morning. It's amazing what fatigue and heat does to your mood and consequently your impression of a place. We were approached by a female backpacker asking for money, claiming she was hungry. She was very pushy but it got her nowhere.

"She doesn't look hungry" I observed, noticing that she looked very well fed.

It might not have been politically correct but it was an honest thought.

We next headed back through some terrible roadworks to re-join Ruta 5 which was as boring as the day before, but served us well for the long ride north to our target town of Chillan. On arrival we caused a bit of a stir having stopped downtown, and soon had a crowd admiring the bikes and asking questions. A friendly couple advised us to head for a place called Pinto, where we would find a good campsite. On arrival we found it was an out of season Holiday Park, expansive but empty. Raymond and Wilson had to head off on the bikes for supplies after we discovered the on-site mini market was extremely mini (i.e. no food, beer or water). I happily guarded the tents and pottered around enjoying the silence. We were well-spaced out (tents not drugs) and had a good sleep that night.

Sat 28/2/15

That morning as we packed a bunch of young Chileans arrived and set up camp. Before long they had the ghetto blaster on at full volume; we had timed things well. Today would be our first ride into a big city despite the fact we had planned to try and avoid all South American cities. We had changed our plan as Santiago had been recommended to us on more than one occasion as we made our way north.

We stopped off at a Shell station just outside of the city to choose a target accommodation. A hotel came up on trip advisor called the CasaSur Charming Hotel, it seemed like a good place to start. The good old Garmin's led us right to it in a back lane down town. For such a large city the ride had been easy with fairly light traffic. We rang the doorbell on the gate and a guy in his thirties came out and greeted us in English with a smile. He explained they were closed until Monday but would check with his wife to see if they could accommodate us. Fortunately his wife said yes and it proved to be a fantastic find.

Sun 1/3/15

CasaSur Charming Hotel turned out to be very charming indeed. Located in a traditional street close to a subway station in Santiago's Providencia district. It had an outside patio, great rooms and a breakfast to die for. Eduardo and Catalina were the perfect hosts. We spend our Sunday doing the tourist hop on hop off bus tour which was actually a great chance to rest. I put the headphones on and actually dozed off a few times. It's not that the tour was boring, it was because I was so chilled. I loved the feel of Santiago with its mix of old and new buildings and was very glad we had not just ridden by as we had originally planned. For me there were no big hit attractions, it was just an overall attractive city with a relaxed atmosphere, complete with healthy looking and friendly stray dogs. We spent that afternoon relaxing at the hotel, drinking Catalina's amazing coffee and chatting to Eduardo.

"The charming CasaSur Charming Hotel"

Mon 2/3/15

Leaving CasaSur was like leaving old friends as we said our goodbyes to Eduardo and Catalina. We were about to make our second Andes crossing and this one we had been advised was a high one. Eduardo had informed us that we were leaving on what was known as 'Mad Monday'. So called due to the large number of people returning to the city after the school break. He recommended we leave our departure until after 10am.

I wanted to see if I could get the parts required to fix my rear mudguard, so we decided to use up some of the time taking the short ride to Santiago BMW. The ride was not as easy as we had anticipated as Raymond's phone had identified the wrong place; fortunately the owner of the wrong place had one of their employees lead us on a scooter the good few miles to the right place. Santiago BMW was a combined car and bike place with as you can imagine bikes taking second place. I was delighted to learn they actually had the part, and in the excitement I got a little confused around the currency. You can imagine how I felt when I discovered a week or so later they had charged me £50 for a little bracket and a bolt. Absolute daylight robbery.

After that we got out of town with reasonable ease, and headed for Argentina. The crossing was superb, all fully paved as expected, and very high at over 12,000 feet. The highlight was a climb up a sheer slope with the road carved into the mountainside, complete with hairpins every half mile or so. On our descent from the Andes Raymond was unlucky enough to be pulled over by a cop for crossing a double white line. I was in the lead with Wilson following for a change. I noticed events in my mirror and stopped around the corner, where Wilson joined me. We did not want to go back and exacerbate things, but grew concerned as time passed by. Finally, after around half an hour we decided to walk back. Just as we set off a cop on a motorcycle was coming towards us and I flagged him down.

"Your friend is just coming" he said and sped off.

Raymond arrived looking agitated and described how he was basically fleeced by the rogue cop, with the threat of a formal charge and a few days wait for a hearing. We had been warned about corrupt cops, but did not expect this would happen in Argentina.

Soon after we arrived in the famous wine region of Mendoza. It was early evening and we hit the town rush hour. It was not the pretty city I envisaged, I had Napa Valley in mind but it certainly was not that, with so many 60's concrete buildings. We found an apartment hotel on the edge and checked in.

Tues 3/3/15

Before leaving CasaSur we had Eduardo call BMW Mendoza to arrange tyre fitting for us. We had already done a drive by the night before to find the location of the BMW dealer, so getting there was easy. We were greeted by Davicito, who was only a few days into his job, but handled us well. We left the bikes in his care and took a cab into the city to look around. I may be a bit harsh in saying my haircut was the highlight of Mendoza for me, but it probably was. It just didn't do anything for me with such a range of dull architecture. Still a good job was done on the bikes and as a bonus they were even washed. That night we headed back into town to enjoy some Mendoza Malbec and our last Argentinian Lomo of the trip.

Wed 4/3/15

We had mapped out a route to a place called the Elqui valley in Chile, one of several recommendations Eduardo had made. The Elqui valley is famous for the production of Pisco (Chile's national drink) and it has the clearest skies on the planet, making it the perfect place to locate observatories. It was a long way so we had identified a little place called Los Palmer, close to the border, so that we could do the border crossing the next morning and have an easy Andes crossing.

The ride up Ruta 40 was not enjoyable as it was in such a bad condition, with corrugations running in line with the road constantly trying to throw our front wheels off course. After the large town of San Juan all changed, with good road surfaces and superb wild mountain scenery. We reached Los Palmer around 3pm and were disappointed to find not much there. We enquired at a fuel station how far the border was, and found it was just a few kilometres up the road. More importantly the guy advised us the border would be closed the next day. There was nothing else for it, we had to press on.

"Our first proud display of Stephen's Deafblind Scotland Banner at the Argentine/Chile Border"

The border crossing was easy despite one officious little prat looking at every page of our passports. Then we had one of the friendlier guards take a picture of us with Stephen's Deafblind Scotland banner and an Argentinean sign located behind us. Not long after the border the road turned to ripeo and we a saw a sign saying over 150 kilometres to the border. This could be a long day. The ripeo turned to roadworks and at some point it was freshly laid brown top soil. How we all stayed upright in that section, I will never know. We were climbing very high stopping often to record our altitude. We let out cheers at 10,000 and 11,000 feet as we continued to ascend. We saw a sign for a tunnel and were mightily relieved thinking the worst was over.

In fact the tunnel was under construction, so there was still no let up. We were all getting cold as we hit 12,000, 13,000, then 14,000 feet. The ripeo was ok, but the drops were sheer and scary. I was having major difficulties with the low setting sun blinding me as I struggled along at the back. We ultimately hit a height of over 15,700 feet which is over five Scottish Munro's (mountains over 3,000ft) on a motorbike, amazing or nuts? Whenever we stepped off the bikes, we were breathless due to the thin air. We finally started to make the descent, which is harder to deal with on ripeo than uphill.

The darkness started to close in and I realised I had lost touch with the others. Thankfully my lights were excellent, but still it felt a bit lonely and surreal as I struggled through the high Andes in the dark. I stopped one time for a moment, just to look around me at the shadowed mountains on either side of me and to take in the stillness and silence of the night. Wilson and Raymond had pulled over further up the road, and we noted that we were probably 10 kilometres from the border, which no doubt would be closed by now. That last 10 kilometres was the scariest ride of my life. It was roadworks most of the way with temporary surfaces. At one point I could see Wilson's and Raymond's headlights ahead in the distance, much lower down than where I was. I wondered if I had taken a wrong turn and if this road might end abruptly with a 'to be constructed' bridge, as they often do. Thankfully I was on the right road but the grip of the tyres was awful, and at times there were sheer drops on either side of me. It was on one of these sheer drop sections that I had a big front-end wobble, and for the first time in my life thought to myself "I could die here". There was nothing for it but to keep on moving forward.

We were all delighted, and I was extremely relieved, to reach the border and astounded to see it was still open. Wilson told me later that the relief on my face as I stepped off the bike was radiating out of me. I later realised I had done the whole crossing on the road mode setting on my bike rather than off-road. Not sure if it would have made a huge amount of difference, but I would have taken any help available.

The guard at the border saluted us and waved us into the office. It was 10pm and the friendly young staff processed us quickly. We understood that they had had word from Argentina that we were crossing and stayed open for us. We hoped there would be accommodation close by but sadly it was 80 kilometres further on.

"What is the road like?" we asked anxiously.

"Perfect Tarmac all the way" the young man said with a smile.

His description was spot on; it was a brand new road winding down from the mountains. Wilson described it as a Moto GP track, he was right, and we hastily made our way to the next town. It was there I noticed my ABS brake failure light was on. I checked the brakes were working (minus ABS) and they were, so we cracked on: I was in no mood to be left behind this time. We entered the town of a Vicuña and soon found a hostel. It was 11pm by now and felt like time for bed.

Thu 5/3/15

We had decided after the efforts of the previous day to reward ourselves with a rest day, and boy did I need it. The Hostel we had stumbled on was fantastic with a separate kitchen, washing lines and secure parking for the bikes. We even managed to convince the lady attending to the rooms to do our washing for a small fee. It's amazing how getting clothes washed quickly becomes such a big focus on a trip like this.

I enjoyed my chill-out day in Vicuña wandering around the square and drinking coffee. Raymond went in search of a local phone sim card, while Wilson and I continued to rely on our pre-paid global sim phones. That evening we took a trip out to an observatory to view the stars. We were driven there along with a bunch of German tourists, up the hill via a rough dirt track. It was a little less clear than it could have been due to a nearly full moon but enjoyable and good value.

"The quiet streets of Vicuña"

Fri 6/3/15

Eduardo had suggested the town of Playa Ingles could be a good stopping off place, it was a decent distance north from where we were so it fitted the bill. The ride through the valley was stunning as we made our way towards the coast. We then tracked the coast north from La Plaz stopping off at a truckers stop for food. We had a great encounter with a trucker who reminded me of my Uncle Alex. He was highly amused by our Spanish and highly impressed by our bikes.

"Bolivia!" he shouted with a big grin, while making a gun sign with his fingers.

The Chilean government seemed to be on a massive road improvement drive; there were serious roadworks going on, aimed at creating additional lanes on the highway. Thankfully the existing lane was kept in place for traffic. We all agreed that the Chilean roads, when complete, were some of the best quality we had experienced.

We passed through the area where the Chilean miners were trapped in 2009. I remember it well as I was working in Belgium with a Chilean guy at that time. We seemed to be the only two in our team showing interest and concern. It was close to my heart having been brought up in a village which had seen its own mining disaster.

Finally we reached what seemed like a mini resort in Playa de Ingles. It had a string of restaurants and bars along a beach. A local biker recommended a campsite which we started to make our way towards but struggled to find. Once again we were picked up on the street by an enterprising apartment owner which turned out to be ok for Raymond and me but not for Wilson and his mosquito friend. We enjoyed some good draft beer that night down on the sea front.

Sat 7/3/15

We left Playa Ingles heading for one of my most exciting destinations, the Atacama Desert. I had seen the famous hand in the desert sculpture in many magazines and books. The desert appeared quicker and continued for much longer than I had envisaged. I loved the colours and the raw emptiness of it. It just seemed to go on forever in every direction. After many miles, towards the north of the desert, we finally came upon the Hand of the Desert sculpture.

It was amazing to finally be there, and I felt incredibly excited. We quickly grabbed some photos, just as a tour bus pulled up. Out spilled a bunch of excited students from many different countries including Canada, France, Norway, New Zealand and the US. At first I thought they would spoil our moment but they actually made things even better with their enthusiasm for both the hand and us.

"The Hand of the Desert"

After that the desert seemed to become very industrial and unattractive: it was getting late and there was no accommodation in sight. We decided to eat in a local restaurant in a small town, then press ahead in the dark to the next big town, named Calama. We did not want to ride in the dark but fortunately the roads were well marked and straight. I was relieved to see the lights of Calama appear in the distance and before long we found the hostel that we had identified earlier. We went for a beer in a bar with the locals that night. Raymond was tired and quickly left us to it. It was an interesting experience with older female bar staff dressed in a sexually provocative manner, and a drunken but friendly local guy latching on to us. We followed Raymond a few beers later.

Bolivia
Route Map

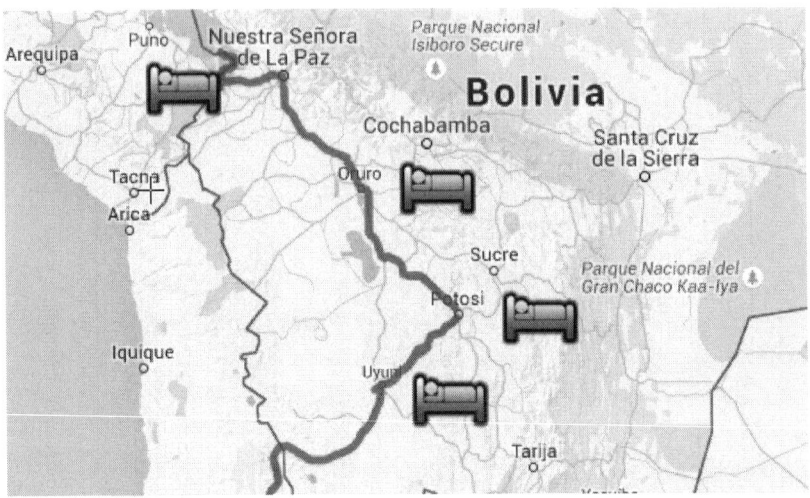

Sun 8/3/15

We set off next morning, Bolivia bound; all feeling a little anxious as we headed towards South America's poorest country. We had chosen what looked like a remote border crossing which Raymond and I hoped would involve tarmac rather than ripeo. The ride out of town created the usual chaos, with many wrong turns and inter-team frustration. Finally we were on our way, on a smooth tarmac road, heading for snow-capped mountains. I could not believe those mountains could be in Bolivia and that I was riding there on my own motorcycle.

After a lot of miles, the perfect tarmac turned to ripeo, then back to tarmac, as we made our way towards the border. The final stretch was extremely poor ripeo, and the town itself had nothing to offer except a rail yard, border post and a stall selling bad coffee and good sandwiches. Wilson was on fast forward mode, and rushing to try to get through the border, while Raymond and I wanted to take some time to suss things out.

"Let's get a coffee and something to eat" I said reeling him back from his quest.

We grabbed some drinks and sandwiches from a kiosk that was just about to close and fuelled up ready for the next stage of our trip.

We processed ourselves out of Chile and rode the short distance to the Bolivian border. We met an unlikely couple of bikers who had teamed up on the road. One was an openly gay and very outgoing Austrian in his late twenties or early thirties, the other a quieter, somehow quaint middle-aged Englishman. They pointed to the huts on each side of the railway line where a train stood with its engines running. The first hut, which was the immigration office, was closed as it was lunchtime, so we hung around in the sunshine. The Austrian guy was in the process of buying some cocoa leaves from the border guards to help stave off any altitude sickness from our up and coming mountain crossing. I tried a bit but was not really enthused by the prospect; I figured I could do without.

The border office finally opened and we were processed fairly quickly for a small fee, for what I am still not sure. The border guys must have done something very wrong to get this gig in a shabby run down office in the middle of nowhere. We then proceeded to hut two, where more stamps were applied and finally, after a visit to the police office, we were free to go. The Austrian had said the road got worse further on, in fact that did not turn out to be the case, at least not the road surface quality.

We were able to make decent time sitting at about 50-60mph on the fairly smooth ripeo. There had been signs of bad weather in the distance as we waited at the border, now it seemed we were heading over the mountains straight into the eye of a storm.

"Bolivian Lama's grazing in the calm before the storm"

We made a quick stop to don our rain gear, then kept moving. When the storm hit us it was like a scene from the end of the world. First it went very dark while the gravel road remained bright, almost white. Then there was lightning forking down, very close to us on many occasions. This was followed by torrential rain, then a hailstorm which coated the road in a few inches of porridge coloured sludge. It was terrifying, but we knew if we slowed down or stopped we would fall. Further up the road had flooded, and in one section there was a strong current to cross. I barked "Keep the power on" across the intercom to Raymond as he moved through it in front of me, remembering the training at Moto Scotland. Thankfully we all stayed upright and we were glad to finally emerge from the tempest in one piece.

After that we seemed to manage to stay just ahead of the weather, though it followed us like a monster. We were left with just the usual challenges; crap gravel and bits falling off my bike (my windscreen extender, which I managed to recover). I was also refused fuel at one of the very few fuel stations on our route. I felt it was harsh in such a remote location, but the fuel attendant would not budge. Thankfully we had been warned that they sometimes don't sell fuel to tourists, so the Rotopax were ready for action. Our second experience of unfriendliness that evening was when a local threw a can of coke at Raymond as he overtook a car. Luckily it missed; no harm was done.

We finally arrived at our destination of Uyuni in the dark. It looked a rundown place, with rubbish in the middle of the streets and dogs scavenging for scraps. Bolivia was living up to its billing as the poorest country in South America. We had a hotel in mind, but were struggling to find it and pulled over to get our bearings.

Two other bikers came across, and greeted us warmly. His name was Andrew, and he was from Vancouver. With him was the young guy from Argentina, Ricardo, whom he had met the night before. They too were struggling to find accommodation. We told him about our hotel plan, but they said they had tried there and it was full. Then we rode in convoy to try another hotel just off the main square. They could only give us one room to accommodate the five of us, so we took it, and were told we could park our bikes in a garage some streets away.

We were joined in the procession (being led by a cyclist) by another biker who was a guest at the hotel. It must have been amusing to see us as we snaked through the streets following the old man on a bicycle. After safely parking up the bikes we all walked back, stopping off for dinner and a good chat. The sixth rider was Marco from Finland, who had been travelling the world for three years on a GS just like mine. He was a cool character, with long blond hair and a great command of English.

Mon 9/3/15

I woke very early that morning, with the four other guys all still sleeping around me. I decided out of decency I would have to wait until 7am before quietly rising. Little did I know there was a time zone change and

7am was actually still 6am. I fumbled for my clothes and accidentally knocked over a coat stand. It was full of heavy bike jackets and crashed noisily to the floor. I acted as if nothing had happened and nipped in for a shower, knowing full well I had woken everyone up. I came out of the bathroom, blasting the room with a loud and enthusiastic "Good morning Vietnam!", to be met with a combination of laughter and groans.

After breakfast and coffee, we collected the bikes and I had a go at clearing my ABS fault. I had had a conversation with Marco the night before. He happened to be carrying a GS-911 unit that can diagnose and clear some faults. He rigged up the unit in the hot sun and cleared the fault, ready for testing. Initially the light remained off, but after 100 yards or so it reappeared. I thanked Marco for trying and packed up ready for the off.

We headed out to the famous Salt Flats on a horrible road with sand, gravel and monstrous pot holes. It blew my mind that the Bolivian government would not want to make this as accessible and attractive to tourists as possible. I guess they were listening though; a new road was under construction a little further along.

"Boris on the Bolivian Salt Flats"

We had been warned by Andrew that the first few hundred yards of the salt road was full of deep puddles. My rear tyre got trapped quite quickly, but I managed to get through ok. Once on the hard salt it was amazing. Just a vast salt desert. A couple of kilometres in there was a visitor centre and a statue in honour of the world famous Dakar rally that holds a stage there. The best bit for me was beyond the visitor centre where there was nothing but the salt, with mountains looming in the far distance. We had a great half hour out there messing around on that vast salt playground. We retraced our steps back to town which included a scary moment where my front end, soft ground induced wobble coincided with a truck heading my way.

In town I stopped and asked a middle aged couple if there was a moto washing facility (in sign language). They tried giving directions but after seeing my blank expression they led us there. It was good to get the bikes desalted although time will tell if the job was totally effective.

After a good lunch stop we headed out of town on a good tarmac road, Oruro bound. We stopped quite quickly at a toll where I was dealt with by a surly female attendant. It was all a bit confusing but she asked for 12 Bov which I duly handed over. We made good tracks for a while, then decided to have a water stop at the side of the road. Wilson was so exhausted that he actually had a few minutes' sleep on the roadside. A biker pulled up and off jumped a very confident young Belgian. He had been touring on a bike he bought locally, and was on his way to Uyuni. He advised us that tolls were free for motorcycles in Bolivia. It was not a lot of money but I was angry that I had been deceived at that last one.

It was dark when we finally made Potosi and discovered that the hostel was very hard to find in this fairly large town built into the mountain-side. We had to ride up some inclines that made the streets of San Francisco look tame by comparison. At one point we took a wrong turn into a road facing downwards on a ridiculously steep slope, where the road then ended. It was one of the most difficult three point turns I have ever made. After much hassle we finally did find the Compania De Jesus hostel recommended by Andrew that morning, and we were glad they had availability. The bikes had to be ridden up a steep kerb, through the front door and into a courtyard. It was not straight forward but we managed with all three of us focusing on one bike at a time.

Tues 10/3/15

We set off the next morning for the destination of Oruno, which would be a staging post towards our final destination in Bolivia, Copacabana, which I still can't say without bursting into song. Unusually, our departure from town was very efficient that morning, or so we thought. I was feeling good, getting into the groove on the twisties just outside of town. We passed a toll booth, this time not stopping to be cheated. A mile or so up the road we came to another nice set of bends. I was unusually positioned in the middle and was just coming out of a corner when a jaggy rock rolled onto the road right in front of me. I tried to react, but had no chance of avoiding it. I knew straight away I had a blow out and shouted down the intercom. The front end went light and wobbly, but I was able to bring the bike to a safe halt.

I moved the bike into the roadside and Wilson and Raymond came up to help. To my despair I had a massive gash in my nearly new tyre, which I was sure would not be fixed with a plug.

"First things first" I said "we have to try".

I took out the kit that we had brought but hoped we would never need. The plug just fell into the gash. As we worked an older English guy turned up on a small trail bike.

"That won't plug" he said, with an air of superiority.

I decided to ignore him and he moved on. We decided the next best course of action was for Raymond and Wilson to take the short ride back into town to try to find someone who would come and pick the bike up.

As the guys rode off I knew I would be there for some time, so I kept myself busy. Luckily although it was hot the sun was being obscured by some wispy clouds. Still I had my cap and my bike balaclava on to protect myself from the strong rays. I sat there conjuring up contingency plans. I had bought a rubber compound that sets hard when exposed to strengthen my IPad cables. I rummaged through my luggage, found it and applied it without any success. First of all the gash was much too wide, and secondly it would never have held the air pressure. A couple of guys stopped in a pick-up truck to see if they could assist, but there was nothing they could do. A herd of Lama wandered past me as I sat there and in some way it brightened my mood.

"This is what adventures are made of", I muttered, smiling to myself.

Another bike came around the corner and there was Andrew, whom we had met in Uyuni, smiling at me.

"What's up man?"

It was good to see him. I showed him the problem and heard for the umpteenth time "You aren't going to plug that".

"I thought you guys were heading for Oruno" he said.

"We are" I replied.

"Well then you're heading in the wrong direction" he was smiling.

Something good comes out of everything. How far might we have gone before we found that out!

I then received a text from Wilson, with the great news that there was a pick-up on its way. After a good couple of hours the lads arrived back.

"The plan has changed" Wilson announced merrily. "The guy wants us to take the wheel back and he will repair it or fit a tyre".

I was surprised to hear he might have a tyre that size, but apparently he had. So after wheeling the bike round on its centre stand to point it uphill (a trick learned from cool Marco in Uyuni) and propping the underside up with rocks, we removed the front wheel.

"Awaiting help in Bolivia"

The guys headed off again and I passed the time sorting out my luggage. A South African guy on a bike pulled over to see if he could assist. He had been travelling for a long time and was telling me about the dangers of Peru where he had had a couple of accidents. He eventually moved on, satisfied I was being looked after. The guys arrived proudly carrying my wheel with a new tyre fitted. "It's a Raleigh Chopper tyre" Wilson said with much delight. He was not far wrong as it was knobbly, not quite the right size, nylon and an unknown Chinese brand. I reassembled the bike and we were on our way back to Oruno. It had been an unfortunate incident but we had worked as a team to resolve it. I felt grateful to my amigos and they felt good that they could help.

We had decided that we all needed to chill in the familiarity of last night's hostel rather than face the unknown of what lay ahead. The tyre felt very weird, making the journey uncomfortable, but I was so relieved the bike was rideable. We arrived back at the hostel and were glad to find we could get our old room back. Wilson suddenly started to look franticly around his bike and rummage in his pockets.

"I've lost the Spot Tracker" he said gloomily. "I think I might have dropped it where your bike was parked, I need to go check".

The thought of going back was a bit of a nightmare as I really wanted to destress but there was nothing else for it.

"I'll come with you on the pillion so I can scour the roads en-route" I suggested.

We did a thorough check, stopping off at fuel stations, the toll and the site of the puncture but with no success. It was a subdued night that night after a hectic and challenging day.

Wed 11/3/15

We set off for the second time to Oruro. Yesterday we had left the city, albeit in the wrong direction, with ease. This morning was different, as frustration built and we stumbled out of town, including me having to brake sharply behind Raymond, nearly losing control of my front end on my new tyre. The first half of the ride was twisty with pleasant scenery, but I was not enjoying it as I lacked confidence in my Chinese off-road orientated front tyre, by a maker that I had never heard of.

The second half was long and straight, and by then I had relaxed into the ride. Oruro was a decent sized town but thankfully finding our hostel was pretty straightforward. I even got my own room, which is always a luxury. I had been thinking about my ABS failure since Chile. I noticed there was damage to my ABS ring so I spent an hour trying to straighten it up, but that did not fix it.

It was market night that evening, and it was amazing to watch people amassing in the centre. There was a railway line right along the middle of the street, and at one time a full sized train came along, prompting the market traders to move their stalls to let it pass. We found a brilliant coffee shop as recommended by the hostel, and had some cracking proper coffee and cake. We had also been advised by the hostel to go to a particular restaurant serving great local food. We searched for it frustratingly for about an hour, finding it only by chance, then discovered it was closed. It was Italian in the square for us that night.

Thu 12/3/15

The ride to Copacabana started out with a long, straight dual carriageway. We had a choice of making a detour at a town charmingly called Ayo Ayo, or heading via the capital La Paz. In the end the choice was made for us as we missed Ayo Ayo. La Paz was traffic madness, with cars and buses coming at us from all directions. It had also warmed up to roasting, and there were long traffic jams. We were delighted that we had not chosen to stay there, and also to finally get out of the city.

After that Bolivia seemed a bit more manicured, as we headed towards Lake Titicaca. We had noticed a gap on the road at a narrow section of the lake and had assumed it was a bridge. Wrong – it was a ferry, but not a ferry as we knew it. It was a flat boat with two rows of uneven wooden planks with holes on either side. It was a challenge getting on, a challenge holding onto the bike on the crossing, and an even greater challenge getting the bikes off. The staff were shouting at us to hurry, which was hard considering it took the three of us to move each bike.

"My ferry bad parking spot"

The little village on the other side would have been a good place to chill for a bit, but we had a good cop/bad cop duo questioning us over the value of our bikes. After the crossing it was a fairly short ride on a recently built road that was already in poor condition to Copacabana.

The town itself was built on a steep slope leading down to the Lake Titicaca which looked like an ocean. The hostel was fairly easy to find, and was a quite grandiose looking building. The owner advised us he had rooms but no Moto parking. There was nothing else for it but to trust them in the street. Thank goodness for the £11 bike covers we had bought from eBay. We had a good night that evening in a restaurant designed to please tourists.

Peru

Route Map

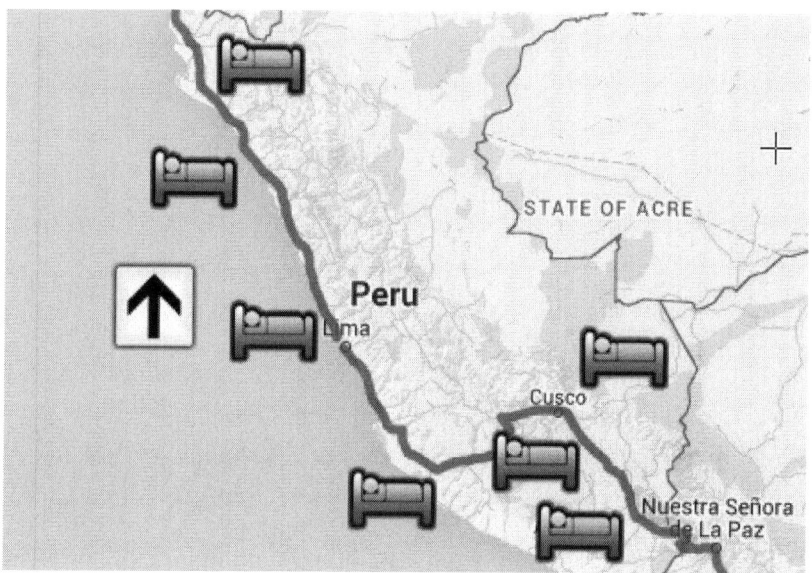

Fri 13/3/15

That morning we all woke up feeling sick. We had indulged in some happy hour cocktails, but this was no simple hangover. Wearily we packed up and headed for the border. The Bolivian side was very disappointing as we had not been issued a form on entry. This meant a 50 Bov payment per head to put it right. We were very grateful to a young man who translated between the official and us. It felt like the second Bolivian rip-off. Still, it was not much money, and my worst fear was that we might be sent back to some office in La Paz. The entry into Peru was the opposite, with friendly officials and a fairly efficient process. Our destination of Puno was only 80 miles further that day, a blessing based on how we felt. We stopped off for a water break, and groaned at the queasiness that rose in waves through each of us.

The hotel was hard to find without a sat nav, but find it we did, and it was great. The owner had us ride the bikes through reception, into the back of the breakfast room. We decided to get a room each based on our growing sense of illness, and went straight to bed. Later that afternoon we connected back, but I still felt like shit and left Wilson and Raymond to go for dinner on their own.

Sat 14/3/15

We woke up to rain and were all still under the weather so made the decision to stay put for another day. I loved the fact I had my own space, and time to relax and recover. Amber was visiting my parents again, so I was able to do a FaceTime with them, which worked really well. Later on I had a good catch up over messenger with Amber as I sat in a café with a hot coffee and lemon meringue pie. I wandered back to my room and watched a Spanish speaking live showing of the England versus Scotland rugby match, which sadly we lost. I was finally feeling better, but still was glad of a quiet night.

Sun 15/3/15

I woke up next morning hoping I had finally shaken off the illness, and to my great relief felt much better. The sun was out and we were ready to set off for our next destination of Cusco. That was after we got our bikes out of the breakfast room, down a massive kerb and onto the busy road. Cusco sits at an altitude 11,000ft, is the Inca capital of Peru, and the staging post for the famous Machu Picchu ruins. This site had been high on our agenda pre trip, but after hearing about the crowds and cost of visiting we had collectively agreed to give it a miss. I was sure Cusco would have some other interesting offerings.

The ride was initially pretty boring and unattractive with a horrible run through a busy market town where it was nearly impossible to avoid the stalls. After that the scenery picked up reminding me of Scotland, including rain into the bargain. The final ride into Cusco was horrible with about 10 miles of suburbs, heavy traffic and crazy drivers. The sat nav seemed to working again as we followed it to its destination, but there was no sign of the hostel. We mucked around for about another hour in the dark before we finally found the hostel back where we had first arrived. It was not obvious at all, tucked away in a courtyard. It was however made up of old buildings, and was very impressive indeed.

Mon 16/3/15

Raymond was keen on exploring the city, and we had pondered an Inca ruins tour bus but none of us could face the tourist trap scenario. Instead we walked to the main square where we had a coffee and checked out the attractions. I had already made up my mind that I was going to work on Boris that day so I would pass on of any sightseeing.

Wilson opted to come with me in search of oil which we finally found at a lube station, which are common in South America. The guy was great and even let me borrow a basin to capture the old oil. The bike was parked under a canopy and there was a big TV box left out for disposal by the hostel entrance. We cut up the box so we could use it as protection on the ground and set about changing the oil and filter. After that I went on to change the air filter, then removed the front wheel to have another go at repairing the ABS ring. I was not confident that it would work. Tomorrow would tell.

I put the old oil into the newly emptied container and took that and the basin back to my new friend at the lube shop. I was a source of great amusement for the guys there as I tried out my Spanish. Once back at the Hostel I left my work place as I had found it. It was overall a very satisfying day.

Tues 17/3/15

The plan for today was to get deep into the Andes on our three-day ride to Lima, Peru's capital, where we would have the other two lad's bikes serviced by a BMW dealer to keep their warranty intact. We had mapped out a plan but this was thrown into disarray in the morning when a German couple advised us that it would be mainly ripeo. We decided we would take Highway 3s instead, infamous for its crazy Peruvian truck and bus drivers. I was disappointed to see my ABS fix had been unsuccessful as the Brake Failure light remained stubbornly illuminated.

As with all Latin American city's getting out was horrible, but after half an hour or so we were amongst the best scenery in Peru so far. Lush green valleys surrounded by mountains, again more akin to Scotland than we had experienced further south. The road was good and soon we were starting to climb further into the magnificent Andes. The temperature started to rise and with it the landscape became starker. Rock falls are common in this part of the world (as I know to my cost) and at one point we had to negotiate around a boulder in the middle of the road which was the size of a small car.

I noticed branches on the road and recalled Joe Laird's comment at our send off in Scotland. He had been on a bike tour in Ecuador and had told us that people leave branches on the road as a warning for traffic accidents etc. There was nothing obvious like that, at least for a while, but there were more rock falls than expected, and soon it became obvious that these were man made.

"The start of the protest road debris"

As we approached a village there were rocks, glass and even logs spread over the road. Cars and trucks had pulled up but we could still weave our way through. We came to the edge of village and debated over the intercoms what we should do next. I had read it can be dangerous to break such protest blockades in Peru, but it was hot and we had no real alternative than to edge forward. We agreed we would ride slowly, no real choice about that, and acknowledge people as we passed. We got into the centre of the village and some people seemed to be warning us to stop, while others waved us on. Finally we were stopped, and sat looking at a crowd gathered further down the street. After around ten minutes a well-dressed man waved us on, so we weaved further on through the street and the crowd. Someone threw a branch in front of me, which I was able to easily manoeuvre past. Raymond had a log laid in front of him which brought him to a standstill until another person ordered the perpetrator to move it away. We were relieved to get away from the situation and left puzzling over what it was all about.

We made another major ascent and descent over a mountain. The roads were very twisty and well maintained, and fortunately there was little traffic. We never stopped to wonder why this was so. As we descended via switchbacks to a major town named Abancay, we started to see the odd rock on the road again, and hoped beyond hope that we were not going back into the protest zone. Sure enough it got dramatically worse as we entered the outskirts of the town.

A pick-up truck full of youths with sticks passed by, and the jeered at us as we smiled and waved. Some people were motioning for us to stop, perhaps looking worried for our safety. I was feeling anxious that we could be heading into trouble, and we agreed to keep moving slowly forward. Once again the alternative of stopping in a restless town was not great. The rubble turned to a few burned out vehicles and there were both jeers and what looked like concern for us from the people in the street. We finally did make it out of Dodge and again were very relieved to be in the countryside.

Ten miles or so further on we came to a long stationary queue of traffic. Our hearts sank as we edged towards the front. There was a major blockade and there were dozens of protesters milling around with sticks and rock launching slings. They had picked a petrol station in a narrow valley with steep cliffs on either side and a fast flowing river to our right. It was an ideal ambush location that I am sure Geronimo himself would have been proud of. They even had people positioned on the cliffs with slings which looked capable of launching stones for half a kilometre.

We pulled up between a truck and a bus and straight away started to generate some interest from the people who were patiently waiting around. A young Dutch girl approached us. She had been traveling around on her own before taking up a placement at a Peruvian animal rescue centre. She explained that the roadblock had been in place from the day before and there was no sign of it clearing. The protest was due to the local government having increased electricity prices to five times the current rate. This was catastrophic for people with so little money, so all of us had sympathy for their cause. A truck driver approached us and indicated for us to leave. He was saying in Spanish that they would let Moto's pass.

We decided to give it a go. I was positioned at the rear. You never know the best position to be in as you approach a baying mob. Number one could get you ripped apart while the others make an escape or maybe number one and two could roar past while they take their revenge on the poor guy at the back. As we approached the crowd surged towards us, mostly wielding sticks. They were shouting at us directing us towards the service station. We had no choice but to turn back and take up our original spot.

"Stuck in a Peruvian road block"

As we waited we got chatting to some guys from Brazil and prepared to wait it out. The young Dutch girl came back and suggested that we could ask if we could pass, using an English speaking Argentinian couple who

99

were on her bus to translate. It was worth a go, so Raymond and I followed the Dutch girl up to her bus where we explained our situation. I was very impressed and grateful that the Argentinian couple were willing to help us. They did not know us from Adam yet they were willing to walk with us into an armed crowd. The lady approached one guy, he quickly pointed us towards the leader, who at that point was doing a rallying speech over a loudspeaker. It felt a bit like walking into the lions' den as we edged through the crowd. We waited until he had finished speaking, then made our approach. The Argentinian couple shook his hand and explained our situation and our fundraising cause. The lead was a small guy, not uncommon for this part of the world, and he had a kind expression on his face. He told the couple that he would let us pass in one hour. We assumed he meant everyone, which was great news. We thanked the couple who had handled the situation brilliantly, and made our way back to the bikes.

While we waited an agitated looking Dutchman approached us. He had been there since the night before and did not believe that they would in fact let us go. He explained he had tried to talk to the protesters the night before to explain that they had a young baby on the bus. He said they were drunk and had hustled him to the ground. He was now afraid he would be seen as a ringleader, so he had called the Dutch Embassy and was awaiting a call back. He advised us to hide our bikes as we might attract too much attention during the night.

It was not looking great, but there was nothing more we could do. Suddenly there was a burst of activity, shouts, engines starting and people running down the road. The road was being opened up. We hurriedly grabbed our gear and within a minute or so were edging towards the epicentre. Everything came to a halt as we arrived just beside the crowd of protesters. At one point they appeared to surge towards us, but thankfully it was just to board a nearby truck to take them home. Slowly the road cleared, and we were on our way. The day was still not over, with 10 miles or so of semi cleared roads and crazy bus drivers. Not surprisingly we did not make our intended destination that day, but did eventually find a cheap hotel with secure parking in a town called Chalhuanca, a hundred or so miles short of our original destination. I lay awake that night for a while mulling over the day's events.

Wed 18/3/15

We were off early the next morning as the hotel did not provide breakfast. Not surprising really at £10 a head. Before long we were climbing up high again. The ascent seemed relentless as we started to enter the cold damp clouds. The temperature started to fall rapidly, and before long we were in single figures. Soon after that the rain came on, it was pouring. It was a horrible combination, a steaming visor covered in rain, steaming glasses, now covered in rain as the visor needed to be lifted, cold body and worse of all a Raleigh Chopper tyre. I kept willing the descent to start, but it was slow to come. We passed through a town on the summit of over 14000 feet, and I asked myself why anyone would build a town there, and indeed, why anyone would want to live there. After what seemed like a lifetime we started to descend from the mountain, and the temperature increased from our record low of 1 Celsius to 17. We finally arrived in Puquio, which had been yesterday's original destination. There was very little to it, so nothing lost. After a really bad coffee we headed out of town to make our next high mountain crossing. This one was equally high but the temperatures remained in the teens. The challenge this time was thick fog and teeming rain. Again it was an extremely long and uncomfortable crossing, with an unfortunate Raymond leading us through the gloom. We finally descended into warm sunshine towards the west coast, and our destination of Nazca. It was so good to be able to ride with a clear visor and warm air buffeting my weary body. Nazca took me by surprise with its manicured square and quality fixtures and fittings. Our sat nav was supposed to lead us to a hostel but lead us instead to the fancy looking Bris hotel. Wilson and Raymond checked it out and found we could have a room each for £20. It was a deal, and a just reward for the struggles of the last two days. I made full use of my me time that evening wandering around town.

Thu 19/3/15

We decided to ride straight to Lima that morning, rather than making another stop. We had been pleasantly surprised to discover it was less than 300 miles away. We re-joined the Pan American again, heading through a desert landscape which made me think of North African countries like Egypt or Morocco. We passed through some big towns one being Ica, where much of Peru's wine is produced.

As we approached Lima the traffic was building but not yet at a standstill. The ride in was a bit manic, but not too crazy and with our sat navs functioning well we arrived outside the door of the unmarked Hostel Tradiciones, which I had discovered on the web earlier. The owner, Angelo Gandullia, who would be in his sixties or early seventies opened a gate and welcomed us in. There was room at the inn and parking (after rearranging his garden a little) for the Moto's. The hostel was set in an area called Miraflores which I had targeted after reading *Pat around the Americas* blog. It was a very affluent area, well looked after, with restaurants and bars. Angelo was bursting with enthusiasm covering topics from Inca water management to where to eat that night. He even set out a menu for us detailing what we should pick for each course. I could tell straight away he was recommending places for a holiday budget rather than an adventure budget, but my two amigos were hooked.

We wandered through the modern streets to Angelo's fish restaurant and followed his menu recommendation with the exception of the soft drink. We substituted that with a delicious Pisco Sour, the national drink of Peru (as well as Chile). Although it was expensive in Peru terms I have to admit it was the most delicious meal of the trip so far. As we walked back to the room that night I sensed my two Amigos were loving all that Miraflores offered, but for me there was something not quite right. I did not want to spend this kind of money, or at least only on special occasions, and it was not how I imagined things would be in terms of an adventure. I had already decided I would opt out of tomorrow's dinner.

Fri 20/3/15

The room we had been allocated was perfect for me as the early riser. Nice low level natural light, no creaky floors or doors and hot coffee available downstairs. For once I was able to get out without disturbing the guys. That morning we had pre-booked the bikes into BMW Lima. Ludwig and Sheila badly needed a service while Boris needed his ABS looked at, broken mudguard bolt drilled out and a replacement front tyre fitted. I had done some research and had also hoped to visit Touratech in Lima to get a replacement bulb for my spotlight. I had noticed Touratech also did tyres, so I was a little unsure which option I would take. The service manager Javier greeted us enthusiastically. I explained what I needed. Drilling out the broken bolt was common practise for them so no issue. The ABS (after a quick diagnostic test) fault was a broken front sensor, but they had none in stock. They had only one suitable tyre in stock which was 50/50 on-road/off-road made by a German company called Heidenau at a cost of $160. I was shocked at the price as I had read tyres were cheaper in Peru. I initially turned it down, but after some deliberation decided it was going to be too hard to do anything based on heat and traffic so I got them to go ahead.

We headed out to another of Angelo's recommendations which was a coffee house selling what he described as the world's greatest rice pudding. The place itself was great, but the rice pudding was way too sweet for me, so my wee Granny Mason's record remains intact as far as I am concerned. I spent my evening chilling on the balcony with some wine and a supermarket platter of chorizo, cheese and olives while the boys hit a nice Italian restaurant in town.

"Raymond chilling in Lima, Peru"

Sat 21/3/15

Angelo had enthusiastically told us that it hadn't rained in Lima for over 2,000 years but the skies looked very dark as we sat in the taxi heading to pick up the bikes. The bikes were lined up in the forecourt all shining like new pins. All the work had been done as promised and my new front tyre was looking awesome. I gulped when I looked at the discarded Raleigh Chopper tyre, thinking I crossed the Andes on that in the wet and rode at 70mph entering Lima. As we made our way back to the hotel the rain came on, splashing up onto our clean bikes. We laughed when we heard Angelo tell the next guests that it hasn't rained in Lima for over two thousand years, well until for this morning.

The ride out of Lima was hell on earth. The rain had been replaced by hot humid sun, traffic was manic and often at a standstill, and we were straying off the highway. After eventually getting to the suburbs and taking an overdue water stop, we all agreed we would call it a day seventy or so miles up the road. We stopped off at the Gran Hotel La Villa in Huacho which was ideal as it was cheap, secure and had a pool to cool us down.

Sun 22/3/15

Our next destination in what was now desert country was Huanchaco, which is a little town on the beach next to the city of Trujillo. The ride was straight forward with a mixture of coast and inland single and dual lane roads. In Trujillo itself we experienced our first moment of getting split up. I was at the back following Raymond around a major roundabout when he took the turn before the one my sat nav was indicating. I guess I could have followed him, but simply muttered "where are you going" to myself and carried on. I stopped after the roundabout for a while, wondering if he would follow, but he did not. I decided to move on and head for the address of a hostel we had put in our sat nav. It was about ten miles or so of city riding, but fairly relaxing. When I arrived I found the hostel but no amigos. I bought an ice-cream and checked for availability, there was none, but I decided to hang around. As always I was figuring out plan B in case of a no show. It was not long before they pulled up, and we were once again three. We decided to look around for another hostel, and found the perfect one just around the corner. It was another expensive restaurant that night, but I stuck to the cheap pasta option. The expense was really starting to get to me.

"Wilson (the only one) enjoying Peru's national drink"

Mon 23/3/15

We were not long out of Trujillo next morning when I spotted another GS sitting behind me. I gave him a wave and he enthusiastically waved back. He followed us for a good while before we were stopped at roadworks. He introduced himself as Jay from California. He continued to tail us for another good fifty miles or so before we pulled in for a coffee stop. He asked if he could join us, to which we said "of course". He had been riding since July on a brand new bike. It turns out his house had burned down back home and he had decided to hit the road for a while. This was his second big South American trip. He was fifty-nine years old, small in stature, but big in vocal volume. I liked him. He asked if he could tag on with us for a bit which was fine by us.

Our destination was Piura which would position us perfectly for getting into Ecuador the next day. Jay found a good hotel in Piura, and negotiated a great rate for two double rooms. That night we struggled to find a place to eat with one place being too loud and fast foody for Raymond, and another being too high end for me. Eventually we found a reasonable local compromise.

Ecuador

Route Map

Tues 24/3/15

A new day and a new country beckoned. Machala in Ecuador was our destination of choice; we felt it was far enough over the border to be in safer territory. As we headed west to join the coastal route north to the border, we pulled up at a garage which served coffee of sorts and took a rest. A 4x4 pulled over and out jumped two guys we had never met, who then proceeded to greet us like old friends. One told us he was half Swiss, half Peruvian, the other was Austrian and they told us that they had set up a biker's hostel in Manorca, the next town along. They had a collection of bikes and a garage set up for small jobs. Had we known about this earlier, we would have definitely made an overnight stop there, but it was too soon to stop there that day. Riding through the town soon after, it turned out to be the best looking beach town we had seen on the trip. So if you're passing I would recommend a stop at Eco Fundo La Caprichosa.

We moved on and arrived at the border around 4pm and had to spend a bit of time trying to find our way around it. For the first time we were directed to make photocopies of our documents at a nearby shop. Jay had gone off in a different direction as we pulled up, so we assumed as he had done it before, he would be ahead of us. After about an hour and a half we were done but there was still no sign of Jay. Eventually he came by, still with the longest bit of the process to do. We were hot and keen to get to our destination before dark so we agreed to meet him at his suggested hotel the 'Grand Americana' in Machala. I felt bad about leaving him, but the thought of hanging around for what turned out to be another two hours was unbearable.

Ecuador was green and full of banana plantations. How can that possibly happen? The Peru side of the border was an arid desert. The drivers were noticeably better and the infrastructure already looked better than Peru also. Within an hour or so we were in Machala, and by luck we quickly came across the Grand Americana. We checked in for a good price and eventually went out for Pizza. There was still no sign of Jay.

Wed 25/3/15

Machala was a clean cut city, very modern, much more so than we had been used to in Peru. As I walked down to reception a hotel worker signalled to me that Jay was in the hotel. He joined us just before breakfast as animated and vocal as ever. He had had a bad night. The customs guy had gone for dinner just as he arrived, they had a printer problem and last but not least he had dropped his bike due to a steering lock issue. I tried to offer some advice, telling him to contact BMW now, I was sure there was a serious fault, but he was all for doing his own thing. As we parted ways he was going to a BMW dealer in Guayquil and we were heading for Vinces. Wilson had suggested we look at bike tour maps for a potential route and Vinces was bang in the middle of one that looked about right.

"Jay"

The ride was slow and sweaty as we made our way past truck after truck on the busy Pan-American. Things quietened down a bit after the Guayguil exit, where we entered a swampland where they were mass producing bananas. We stopped off at a little restaurant for some delicious local chicken soup and the best banana I have ever tasted. Talk about fresh!

Vinces was a bit of a disappointment; it was a bit run down and we had no idea where to find a hotel. Eventually we stopped in a poor part of town to discuss our plans. Within seconds we were surrounded by locals which was pretty intimidating but it soon became clear they were friendly, just wanting pictures of us and them with the bikes. We asked about a hotel and one guy who looked like the local boss man offered to lead us there in his car.

The Rizz Hotel had seen better days but was perfect for the night, and was set on the river. The owner explained that VInces was famous for its chocolate production and pointed out a factory from his roof top terrace. He arranged a taxi to take us to a traditional restaurant where the local football was showing on TV. Bliss.

Thu 26/3/15

I had a restless night as I was conscious that it was my father's 84th birthday next day, and I wanted to contact him while Amber was there to help with FaceTime. That would be just after 6am my time. I tried FaceTime but it failed. I followed that up with a call that was soon cut off. Finally I managed to get them on Skype audio, which worked just fine. It was good to hear he was enjoying himself.

After that it was time to eat. The hotel owner had sourced some pure local chocolate for us, and had made it into a frothy drink served along with a good breakfast. We really appreciated that he had gone out of his way to do that for us.

Next we had two choices on our route up north; mountains or coast. My choice would have been mountains, but I lost out to the coast. The road to Canoa was not long in distance but as we had already found in Ecuador, travelling was slow and extremely hot. We pulled up in Ecuador's surf town early evening and found a good hostel with a room each. We would spend two days here chilling. Canoa can only be described as 'up and coming'. It's got the basic ingredients of a fantastic beach with a sea as powerful as I have experienced and sunshine. It's also got a great new road leading to it. Other than that it's pretty much a South America type shambles. Still I liked it.

Fri 27/3/15

I had a magical day of solitude walking into town for coffee and cake, writing up my journal, swimming in the pool and drinking a beer on the porch outside my room. That night I wandered down to one of the many beach bars and watched the sun set. Raymond soon joined me and we celebrated with a fine Cuban cigar that he generously provided. Wilson came looking for us, but somehow our ships passed in the night.

"Sunset in Canoa"

Sat 28/3/15

Today we would head for Santo Domingo just south of Ecuador's capital Quito. This was the best ride so far in Ecuador with quiet sweeping roads. We were on the hunt for the equator that morning. In the usual inexplicable South American way, Ecuador had managed to hide what we thought should be a major tourist attraction. We actually had to back track seven miles to find the totally unassuming sign, situated on a nasty bend in the road.

We had finally reached a major milestone, having ridden half way up the planet.

I expected to be climbing high into the mountains that day as Quito is positioned at 9,000 feet and we would be only about seventy miles short. We did climb but it was more gradual, feeling more like hills than mountains, and very scenic all the same. Then we rode into Santo Domingo, not a pretty city, and found a cheap room in the Torreazul Hotel which turned out to be great value. The lads later informed me that they thought it was a 'short term let' for sex hotel. I must admit I hadn't noticed a thing.

We had our first Chinese meal of the trip that night, and based on quality it would be our last.

Sun 29/3/15

I woke early again that morning, pondering my faulty ABS. Could I have damaged the cable when replacing the air filter? Must check, I decided. Today's destination had extra significance. My daughter Stephanie had spent three weeks there with a friend and her family. The girl had spent time in Stephanie's high school in Cumbernauld, Scotland, which was quite different to Quito, I would imagine.

Now that we were rapidly approaching Columbia, I decided to check the FerryXPress website to check out sailing days. I immediately spotted red highlights on the March and April schedules, with some sailings cancelled or at risk of it. The confirmed sailings were now only once a week, leaving us a choice of the 7th or 14th April. My rough schedule had us leaving Columbia on the 9th of April. The 16th would put us under too much time pressure, so we had to go for the 7th. That meant we would have more flexibility north of the Darien Gap, probably a good thing. Cutting

Columbia short was disappointing; we had really been looking forward to it. Based on this new development, I suggested we miss out Quito and head further north, staging us for an earlier entry into Columbia. We agreed to head for Ibarra, north of Quito and cross the border the next day.

As always in South America, expect the unexpected. Just outside Santo Domingo we were stopped by the police who informed us that the main route north was closed due to landslides. Fortunately for us there was a fork on the road which took us roughly in the same direction. The ride was wet and slow due to the diverted traffic, but after a while we hit the north-east corner of Quito. It may have been because it was the more affluent section of town, but I was very impressed by what I saw. The place looked modern and well organized, there was an air of prosperity and refinement that was very different to most of our recent experiences.

On arrival in Ibarra we found the Hostel El Portal, which 'Pat of the Americas' had recommended. It was a great choice although somewhat marred by noisy kids still running around at 11pm. The town itself was fine, though not pretty, and was well situated for our border crossing the next morning.

Columbia

Route Map

Mon 30/3/15

The ride to the border was eighty miles of great mountain twisties, in mainly dry weather. There had been no breakfast at the hostel, so the first priority on arrival was finding something to eat. There were a few small basic cafes, so we chose one where we could keep an eye on the bikes. The grumpy woman owner served us scrambled egg with boiled rice, which was actually pretty good.

The border process was fairly easy after a bit of questioning and wandering around. The slowest bit was waiting for photo copies, where we also had to constantly defend our place in the queue. We asked about insurance, but were told it was not available at the border. This was of slight concern as we entered our sixth country.

Initially Columbia looked the same as Peru, but before long the scenery improved big time with amazing deep gorges and good quality roads. The border crossing had taken three hours in total, so we decided we would stop at the first city en-route, which was Pasto. It was a chaotic place with chaotic drivers, and it was now raining heavily as we searched for a hotel. We ended up getting nowhere, so decided to head towards the next city and look for a hotel on the way.

On our way out we noticed that the outskirts of Pasto started to look a lot better, so we stopped and tried the sat nav for a nearby hotel. The hotel Frances La Maison was first on the list, and we headed for that. As per the now routine process I let Raymond and Wilson go and check it out. I was still concerned about cost and it looked a bit upmarket. They came back grinning, saying it would work well with a single and double room available at a reasonable price. We were greeted by a wonderful French guy named Patrice who welcomed us into his small, cosy French country style hotel. The bikes were garaged in a lockup just across the street, and it was Wilson's turn for the single room. It turned out to be an excellent choice and a really nice part of town.

I still had not been told the actual price, so I checked the tariff table on a notice board outside my room. I calculated it would cost about £50 each. My heart sank; this was all getting too expensive. Then I listened as Raymond asked Patrice for directions to the best restaurant in town. I was on edge as we set out to look for it. When we did eventually find it, a few wrong turns later, it looked high end.

I finally cracked and said

"No way, I can't afford to do this trip at this level of spending. We're already in a £50 each hotel which is too expensive, and there's no way I am adding this to it".

The two Amigos declared it as no problem, and we headed up the road to a local cheap but perfectly good restaurant.

We had a good 'clear the air' conversation that night. Raymond said that he had not realised I was on a set budget, and explained that when he was asking for the best restaurant he had not meant the most expensive. He talked about how he thought we were moving too fast in our schedule, not taking enough in. Wilson confessed that he was frustrated because the bike pace was too slow for him, and that he felt we were not having enough fun. I said I have one goal regardless of pace, speed or fun,

"I'm going to Alaska".

Not sure we resolved it that night, but we did agree that Wilson should take off in front of us when he wanted to, that we would try and schedule more stops of longer than a day, and that I was going to Alaska regardless of any of that.

Tue 31/3/15

It turned out that the hotel somehow worked out at around £27 each, which was a bargain. After another round of photo shots with kids, parents and grandparents outside the hotel, we headed north. We were only minutes into the journey when Wilson announced that he had a warning light on. The warning light turned out to be a tyre pressure issue, and on inspection he found a nail in his rear tyre. Amazingly there was a Goodyear garage a few hundred yards up the road, where it was plugged straight away.

The road to our next destination was again fantastic, with the initial part being similar to the previous day. Around half way the gorges were replaced by green lush valleys and straighter roads. We noticed that there was a high military presence at strategic places, such as bridges.

It was getting dark as we approached Cali, which is a big city with over 2 million inhabitants. Traffic was once again manic as we made our way to the hostel we had identified earlier. We got close to the hostel, but could not locate it. Luckily. A French ex pat woman eventually helped us to find it. Raymond came back from an initial foray to tell us that there was no answer at the door, and that the sign said 'minimum stay two nights'. The French woman then walked with Raymond, showing him where there was another hostel. It always amazing to find just how helpful people can be.

The Hostel San Fernando was available, and actually better located. An anxious looking American woman checked us in, while her Columbian husband sorted out the parking of the bikes. We dined that night in a local hamburger joint, also recommended by the French woman; I am so glad we did as it was absolutely delicious. When Raymond called it a night after eating, I decided to try and up Wilson's fun meter, inviting him for a few more beers in the square. We ended up soaking in the carnival atmosphere till late. It really was fun.

Wed 1/4/15

Turns out the Columbian husband is a cool character who collected classic convertible cars. He has a Bobby Ewan Mercedes and a wartime Ford under wraps in his yard. He walked us down to a very local breakfast kiosk, placed our orders and left us to enjoy it.

We asked him about insurance which is known a SOAT in South America. After phoning around he found us a place that would do it. He ordered a cab for us and after an hour we were covered. It was a great relief.

"Our cool Columbian host"

Today's destination was Salento which had been recommended to us by Andrew the Canadian, whom we had met in Bolivia. It was located right in the heart of the coffee region. Raymond and Wilson were talking about a coffee plantation tour but I was not sure if I wanted to join them. It was a short ride, just over one hundred and twenty miles on mainly dual carriageway roads. The little town was clearly a tourist place but it was enjoyable. It had a steep street lined with gift shops, restaurants, coffee shops and bars. The square had tents offering food and drink with Latin music blaring out from every corner. Our hostel had an underground car park with a ridiculously steep slope which was scary to go down, and we did not relish the prospect of getting back up.

My best memory of the town was the coffee and the lemon cake we bought from the Jesus Martinez café. Both tasted like the best we had had on the trip so far. We had dinner later that night which ended on a sour note with a heated skirmish between us. I was glad to have a room to myself that night.

Thu 2/4/15

The ride up the ridiculous slope took us directly onto a narrow street. One of us was positioned to check the road was clear, the other to signal to the rider and the third to ride up and out. In the end we all managed to get up and out safely.

The road to Medellin started out with slow traffic through big towns, then a tough mountain crossing followed by a boiling hot river valley. After that it was another gruelling mountain crossing and then we were there. All in a days riding in South America. Medellin is Columbia's second largest city, with around 3 million inhabitants. Medellin was infamously the most dangerous city in the world, and the home of Columbia's drug lord Pablo Escobar. Thankfully the city has cleaned up its act recently. Wilson had identified a biker friendly pub which did accommodation, and was run by a Scotsman. It had been an Irish pub but had rebranded itself as 'Busters'.

Wilson was ahead of us, and was sitting outside as Raymond and I pulled up.

"It's basic but cheap" he said.

It was a spot on description, so we checked in and unloaded our gear. The Scotsman, Al was not around but he would be in later. His business partner was a Canadian in his thirties, who was running adventure activities out of the premises. We didn't meet Al that night, as we were out when he called round. He would be back in the morning for a coffee.

We had another first that night. We rode our bikes into the pub before going to bed while there were paying customers in the bar.

Fri 3/4/15

As promised a larger than life Al from Lanark arrived the next morning and we chatted, well mainly Al chatted, over coffee, for a good few hours. He was into gold mining and had spent some time in Ecuador before moving up to Colombia. He was a colourful guy and clearly really enjoyed being with people from the old country. He told us about the boom and bust times and how his pub was now struggling. He also told us about living in Medellin itself. We had completely lucked out as we were there on Easter Friday and most of the city had gone to the countryside for the break. It was nothing like the manic South American cities we had become accustomed to. Al also told us that many Americans visited there to pick up young 'trophy' girlfriends who expected to be lavished with gifts in return. For that reason 'Gringos' had a bad reputation here. When Al left the lads decided to go for lunch, while I decided to take the chance of some time on my own.

I wandered around the quiet streets feeling a bit uncomfortable that I might be taken for a sex tourist or Gringo. The rain came on hard as I waited for Raymond back at the accommodation at the agreed time; unfortunately he was holding the keys. When he didn't show up I suspected they had found wine and were unwilling to face the rain. It was several hours before we finally met up again, and by that time I was royally pissed off. Time to count to ten.

Wilson noticed from Facebook that the *Two Wheeled Nomads* were in town. Jason and Lisa were an English couple who had been on the road for many months during which time we had been following their posts online. Wilson tried to set up a get together, but as we were on the other side of town it did not work out, which was a pity.

Sat 4/4/15

We all woke up tired after a disturbed sleep. Too much music and comings and goings in the pub that night, although I had missed the worst of it. Apparently there had been a guy banging on the metal doors in the middle of the night. Wilson and Raymond thought we were under attack, but it turned out to be a drunken guest. It was time to move on.

Our next destination, Caucasia, was basically a stopover point, just under half way to Catagena, where we would catch our ferry. We spent another frustrating time trying to get out of town with several wrong turns before finally finding the right route. Al had informed us that the first part of the ride was similar to the busy twisty mountain route we had crossed on our way in. Wilson was out front enjoying himself, with Raymond and I following at a more leisurely pace. The rain came on, then off again, but still it was warm and humid. We stopped for shade at one point, unintentionally next to a little local one-woman café. It was a good opportunistic find as we badly needed to rehydrate.

We joined Wilson further up the road, and stopped off for a break. A heavily armed young soldier approached us, wanting to look at the bikes. We had a friendly encounter with him, taking photos and trying to make conversation. We were to hear a few weeks later that the army was attacked in that area by FARC (Fuerzas Armadas Revolucionarias d Colombia, a terrorist organization) resulting in loss of lives. I hope our young man survived.

"Chatting with a friendly young soldier"

We were on the final stretch to Cuacasia when I noticed two British plated bikes by the side of the road. I recognised the bike and rider at the back. It was Lisa and Jason from the *Two Wheeled Nomads* whom we had tried to connect with the day before.

I shouted over the intercom to Raymond, who was ahead of me, to let him know. We were already a bit past them, and the road was narrow, so we decided to keep going. We could catch up to Wilson and flag Lisa and Jason down further up the road.

Wilson was waiting for us just outside Cuscasia where we headed into a fuel station. Knowing that Jason and Lisa were behind us, we agreed to wait and flag them down. Around 15 minutes later they arrived and pulled over to where I stood waving by the side of the road. We had a great chat then Jason suggested we go to look for a hostel together. We finally ended up in a Hotel that Al in Medellin had told us houses U.S. Drug Enforcement Agents. It was a built in a U shape with gates on the open side. It had great rooms and perfect parking for the bikes, and as long as there wasn't a drug cartel gang attack in the night we would be fine.

We ate out that night with Jason and Lisa, enjoying a great night with the two adventurers. I loved the combination of high octane Lisa and down to earth Jason. There was no drug cartel attack that night, but we were assaulted by the air conditioning which was left on far too cold; the remote control went missing in the dark.

Sun 5/4/15

Now we were five as we made our way to Catagena, our final destination in South America. Jason led the pack at a nice steady pace, and after an hour or so he pulled over at a juice bar. This was a novelty for us as we normally looked for coffee shops. The guy serving was a real character, full of smiles and taking the time to show us his collection of model ships. As we headed north, I found myself separated from the pack due to conflicting sat nav routes, I decided to stay relaxed, I knew I would find them somewhere up the road. Then Wilson appeared, telling me that he had been sent to find me.

We tried to reconnect with the others, but failed. It was a 220 mile ride, a lot in the stifling heat and heavy traffic. The crazy bus drivers were at it again. I later learned that the drivers are financially incentivised to drive fast and work long hours. They are basically racing each other to be first at the next bus stop. There had been a bus crash recently in Peru that killed 37 people. I waved Wilson on; I wanted to ride at my own pace.

I noticed in this part of Columbia that it was common practise for cafés to blast out music at a crazy volume, even crazier than the South American norm. That combined with a lot of youths hanging around gave it an intimidating air which I had not experienced further south.

Wilson and Raymond were waiting for me at the roadside just south of Catogena, while Jason and Lisa had headed on into town to find the Irish friends that they had met on the road. We tried to find Jason and Lisa for a while, but as it was getting dark we decided to look for a hostel. There was an area in the sat nav where a lot of hostels were showing up, but it turned out to be really seedy. The stress of the search raised team tensions before we finally found the Hotel Mariand Plaza after a couple of failed attempts. It was cheap and basic but would do the job. We booked three badly needed single rooms to chill out. Catogena surprised me in that it was a big city. I had visions of a small port town but it was huge.

Mon 6/4/15h

Our first priority next morning was getting the ferry paperwork sorted out. It was not like boarding a channel ferry here, there was always paperwork to be done. Of course our FerryXpress confirmation gave us no indication of that. Thankfully Jason had alerted us to this fact, which I had followed up on the forums. We took a taxi to a shipping agent company called Roza. Taking a taxi was not straight forward. The first guy looked at our instructions and simply said no. The next guy was much more helpful. He called an English speaking friend, who talked to Wilson on the phone and translated our requirements. The process in Roza was straight forward after handing over our passports, temporary vehicle import documents, Soat (insurance) and V5. For a fee of $25 they handed us back three sets of documents including photocopies and we were good to go. I had read we should then go to customs but the English speaking lady said no need.

After that I wandered along to the local shopping centre in search of a badly needed beard trimmer. I found one but felt at around £30 equivalent it was a bit pricey, and ended up buying some cheap hairdresser's scissors instead. They actually did not a bad job and for the first time in a long time I was looking tidy. I vowed I would buy a proper trimmer in LA.

For one of the first times on the trip we played tourist, taking a taxi down to the old town. It's a walled city, due to the fact the British kept attacking it and stealing its gold. Catogena was the major port for moving gold back to Spain. Apparently Prince Charles recently unveiled a plaque to all the British sailors (pirates?) who were killed at sea. With some justification the locals defaced it soon after.

The old town itself was beautiful, with many grand old buildings and churches. It was nice just to chill in the plaza with a great tasting coffee that afternoon. That night we took a taxi back in to the old town to meet Jason, Lisa and their Irish friends Mike and Orla. They were on a South American trip, two up, on a BMW GS650. Mike was a typical confident Irishman from Galway who did contract diving work in Australia. Orla was a petite Irish lass with a lot of spirit. I chatted to them about Galway, a place I spent a long time in during my early work years. No Great Southern Hotel, no Corrib Hotel but Moran's Fish Restaurant had survived. I liked Mike and Orla, and loved their sense of adventure. It was nice to have a larger company and I think all three sets of travellers enjoyed the craic.

"Jason to the left of Wilson, Mike to the right with Lisa sitting behind Orla"

Tues 7/4/15

We were told to be at the ferry port by 11am so we had agreed an 'engines on' time of 10am. We tried repeatedly to put the port address into our sat nav but failed. It was 10:20am by the time we left, not completely sure where we were going. Considering we had paid over £300 each and there was not another ferry for a week, I naturally felt a little anxious. I looked at my sat nav and if I zoomed out a little I could see the shape of the port. I suggested the others try this too, and it worked well. Fifteen minutes later we were rolling into the port.

There were a couple of bikes already parked up, and one approached us as we pulled up. The guy was very animated, telling us that they were trying to charge $35 for fumigation which was a rip off. He was asking us to join with him in refusing to pay it. We were in the process of recovering from the stress and heat, and had been made aware of the charge, so were not interested. Another guy told us he would do the fumigation, but not until we had taken our bikes across the road to a garage to have them washed. The washing process took an hour and a half, slowed down a bit by a South African family butting in on the process with a large land rover. They were a family of four, living out of their truck, with no intention of stopping travelling any time soon. I liked them, but I did not like that the guy was behaving underhand, pushing in and picking up the hose the guy was using on our bikes. I had begun to get used to it on this trip. I was amazed how pushy South Americans are in queues. I sometimes think I am in Germany or the Netherlands where people in queues often behave in a similar way.

With the bikes washed, the 20 second, $35 fumigation process started. We were now a small community with a wealthy Canadian couple we had met at the Roza office, an American guy from New Hampshire, a Spaniard on a motorcycle, an El Salvadorian biker living in Miami (who earlier protested the cost of fumigation) and the pushy South African guy and family. It was roasting hot with hardly any shade, so we were grateful when they finally ushered us forward into a covered seated area with fans. They also pointed to a mini market, where we were able to pick up some provisions, including cold beer. We had a great chat with Mike and Lorraine, the Canadian couple. They looked as if they were in their fifties, possibly retired, and were travelling to some more adventurous places while they were "still fit", as they put it. He had been in the military, and she in finance, both successfully I would imagine, based on their travel plans. Five star all the way. It was a pity they would not be home in Vancouver when we passed through as they had an eight-bedroom house to share with us.

Finally after about eight hours since arrival we were directed to board the gleaming FerryXpress. It was like entering the modern world again, all polished, bright and air conditioned. It was even better based on the fact it must have been running at about 25% capacity, so there was tons of space. I walked outside and took my last look at South America, and reflected on the tremendous experience it had been. It had not been easy but well worth it.

Panama

Route Map

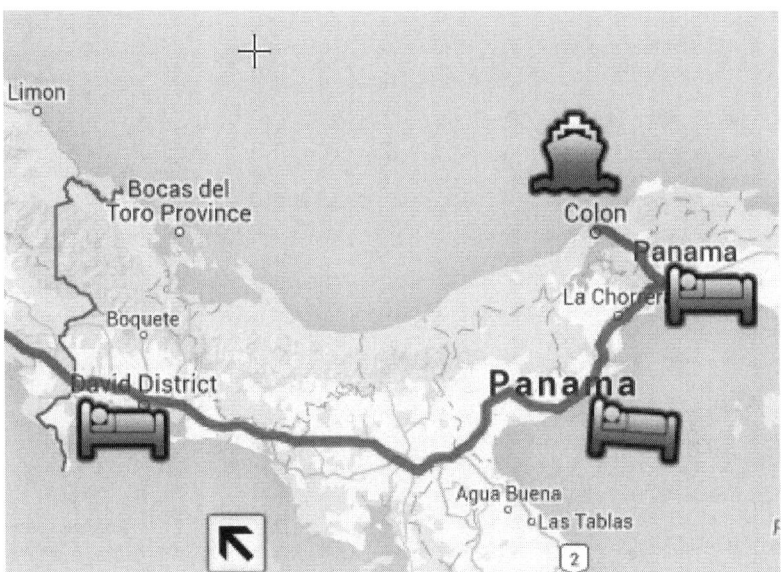

Wed 8/4/15

I had a great sleep that night, calmed by the gentle throbbing of the ship's engines. When I woke I slipped out before the others to grab a cup of coffee. We were well on our way to Panama and a new continent, and I sat enjoying the solitude. We docked earlier than expected, and were soon waved off the ferry. The little community was ushered to passport control, followed by the sniffer dog check and then around to customs, where all efficiency came to an abrupt halt. The delay started when they told us that it would take an hour to get our mandatory insurance because of computer problems. When that was finally resolved it took over half an hour per person to process us in what was clearly a chaotic office.

German, the guy from El Salvador, and Ricardo the Panamanian had suggested we all ride to Panama City together. German had previously stayed at a cheap hotel with good parking. That sounded perfect to us. Ricardo revealed to me that he had been diagnosed with Parkinson's disease, and that he had bought his Harley in his words "to live his life". We finally got released from customs about 7pm, and headed into the setting sun towards Panama City.

Panama looked very modern with big hotel chains and a good road network. Ricardo led us at a very slow pace, sometimes as little as 40mph. It took as an hour or so to reach Panama City in the dark where we pulled into a fuel station to check on the hotel directions and say farewell to Ricardo. The guy had hung around for at least an extra two hours to ride with us. We really appreciated his patience and assistance. German then led us to the Hotel Via Espana, which was ideal. The price was good, with secure parking and a restaurant serving simple food. It also turned out to be close to the Polaris dealership, where we would meet Wilson's friend's son Rafael Jr.

"Ricardo from Panama in Panama awaiting customs clearance"

Thu 9/4/15

German had left by the time we had breakfast. He was off to check if he needed police permission to exit the country and head north. Apparently he had needed permission heading south. Wilson contacted Rafael Jr., who would be our host for the next few days. Rafael invited us to come over to his fledgling Polaris dealership as soon as we were ready. We decided to hang around the hotel for a while making full use of the air conditioned rooms, it was a brutally hot and humid day, eventually heading over to Rafael's shop. We found it with ease.

First to greet us was Diego, Rafael's cousin followed by Rafa himself. Rafa was quiet and thoughtful, Diego was boisterous and outgoing. Rafa had also brought in Tyler, a mechanic from his previous business in Phoenix. Tyler was 22 and a typical young American who called us all 'dude'. The business was still in the process of getting established, with contractors still working on the lighting. You could see Rafa's vision of a rugged outdoors theme coming together. We hung around for most of the afternoon; as usual the work was running behind, but eventually we were ready to go and set out in convoy.

Our trip through Panama City coincided with a meeting of the leaders of the Americas, including Barack Obama, and shortly after we left we were held up at a road closure while some dignitary was whisked through. After that Wilson asked Rafa to pull over at the Panama Bridge for a photo. We crossed the bridge and pulled into a place decorated in a Chinese style, but then were ordered to move on by heavily armed police. I was the last to try and join the traffic, which was streaming down the highway at pace. The only way to get on was to gather as much speed along the short ramp and go for it, which I did.

Just as I joined a mini bus screamed up the side of me and then swerved violently into me. I was instantly thrown into the air, landing on my shoulder and rolling towards the gutter. As I went I was yelling at Wilson through the intercom,

"Some arsehole has hit me"

I knew immediately that I was not injured, so my attention turned to poor Boris, who was lying on one side on the highway. Wilson and a cop had by now stopped, and we lifted him up and wheeled him off the road. Boris had a smashed headlight unit, indicators, speedo face and scrapes on the badges on either side of the tank. The force of the crash had flipped him hard onto each side. Amazingly he still looked rideable.

"Boris down – my toughest moment of the trip"

The mini bus had pulled up, and the cop started proceedings. I was clearly at a disadvantage as the cop spoke no English and I had nada Espanola. The cocky driver was in his thirties and had some English. His passengers, who were gringos, were whisked away minutes after the incident. It turns out they were US security, maybe FBI or CIA. Raymond had continued en route, to try and stop Rafa and the guys. I texted him saying

"I'm good but I need a translator"

They had closed the road again soon after my crash, and at one point a cavalcade of heavily armed vehicles, including guys on motorcycles with sub machine guns, rushed past. I wonder if Barak said

"Hey there's Stevie Mason"

By now it was all getting a bit intimidating; we were the only people left on the road.

The road eventually reopened to the welcome sight of Raymond with Diego on the pillion. At last I felt I had a fair chance. Diego was brilliant, establishing straight away that the arsehole was also a liar; he was saying I had ridden into him. He also established that the arsehole had formed a good relationship with the cop. The big problem I now had was with documentation. We had all bought mandatory insurance at the border. Mandatory meaning you can't get into Panama without it. The problem was that the inefficient/corrupt customs people who had taken hours processing us did not give us back our insurance certificates. Diego argued for at least an hour that we had to be insured as we were here. Finally the cop asked for me for my keys saying he was going to keep my bike. Diego asked me for my travel insurance document, which he presented to the cop. The cop looked unimpressed, but I think he wanted to get this wrapped up, so he finally accepted it. We were free to go.

I was running on adrenaline at this point, and the thought of riding another 50 miles to the beach house, mainly in the dark, with some of it off road, was not a good one. Amazingly my broken headlight still worked. I sat in the middle, with Raymond following the truck and Wilson behind me. I reflected on the incident and wished I had pulled out earlier, later, or that we had not stopped at all. I knew it was not worth the thoughts, if it's going to happen it will. I was still alive and Boris was rideable so I had to move on.

We stopped off halfway to the beach house to pick up provisions. I waited outside, checking Boris over but thankfully I could find no further damage. Tyler stayed with me and assured me we would get it fixed. The last little bit of road to the beach house was rocky, but I managed ok. I had a beer in my hand almost before I was off my bike, and downed a good few more that night.

We had a good night with the guys laughing and joking. They admitted they were pretty apprehensive that three old guys were about to ruin their weekend, but then agreed they were having a great time too. We discussed my next move. Diego would chase customs on Monday for our insurance policy numbers as it was a holiday weekend. Meanwhile we would also get out of Panama on Monday. There was a lot of joking that night about Steve's run for the border. I did not feel bad about that, but I did feel bad at the thought of trying to get Boris in shape to make the next half of the trip.

Fri 10/4/15

I woke up next morning feeling down, my head full of 'what ifs'. The guys were going spear fishing, but I was in no mood to join them. It was a pity because the place was literally a tropical paradise. The house was expansive, with gardens rolling down towards the cliffs above the beach. There was an infinity pool, a hammock area and an endless supply of beer. There were steps leading down from the house ending up at a boathouse by the pristine beach. It was truly amazing.

I spent the time rechecking Boris and generally lazing around. I wanted to go look for parts, but that would have to wait until tomorrow. We had a quiet evening after our over indulgence the night before, and Diego promised to take me to look for parts in the morning.

Sat 11/4/15

The long awaited trip for parts began next morning. We drove about 10 miles to a nearby town where we picked up aluminium tape, connectors and led lights. There were no motorcycle indicators available so we were going to have to make our own. Tyler and I started to brainstorm the options. I suggested a cigar tube for a stalk, and a bottle top for a cover. The design now agreed, the work commenced. It was a godsend having Tyler to help me get it done; I would have struggled with the electrics on my own. I started creating the new headlight using my headlight protector and aluminium tape, while Tyler wired up the indicators. We were whooping USA style when they finally worked. I also had to tie wrap my windscreen tight and used a plastic jar lid to seal my broken speedo glass, but Boris was ready to go. Would the indicators stay on or even more worryingly would the plastic headlight protector be able to handle the heat from the HID light? I would only find out once on the road. I started to look for long term solutions by emailing BMW dealers in El Salvador, Mexico and Los Angeles. Worst case I could have Amber bring me the parts to LA.

"Tyler fixing Boris"

"Cigar Tube Indicators"

That night we all sat down at the beach drinking beer and eating freshly caught fish. The guys were having a great time but I was still struggling. I reflected on how fast that minibus was travelling and how hard he had hit me. I was a lucky man. I wondered how it would be getting over the border, the durability of my repairs and the long term cost of fixing it all. I kept telling myself it's done; I have to move on.

Sun 12/4/15

Sunday was truly a day of rest. I did nothing but chill, read and write and ponder on the road ahead. We had decided to ride to David in Panama to ensure we were set up for the border crossing the following morning.

"Diego in front (Chief Negotiator) and Rafa (Chief entertainment officer)"

Diego, Rafa and Tyler left that evening for the city. We could not thank them enough for their amazing hospitality. Later that evening Raymond called a shipping agent in Oz regarding shipping Sheila home. He was advised it would cost him half the price if he shipped it from LA instead of Vancouver. Getting back to Vancouver from Prudhoe Bay, Alaska was going to be tight, getting to LA was a nonstarter. I wondered, based on this, if the trip for Raymond might soon take a new turn.

Mon 13/4/15

It was a nervous run up to David for me next day. I was worried we would be stopped by the police, as we had been told they often pull over bikers. If they did would they see my repairs and find me on their system? I was worried my repairs would not hold out. Would the cigar tube indicators shake off or would the HID bulb melt the plastic and tape? Was the bike actually running straight? I had been fuelled with adrenaline the last time I rode it and couldn't be sure.

The good news is that after several checks the repairs were holding out, and the bike was running well. As for the police checks, about an hour into our journey a cop signalled Raymond to stop, then me, but in a panic I just waved back at him hoping he might think I misunderstood his signal. A few miles further on we were stopped by a cop in the middle of the road. My heart sank, and I could feel the sweat on my forehead as I pulled up. He told us in Spanish that we had failed to stop for a policeman, and that we would be ticketed. We showed documents and tried to explain it had been a mistake. Fortunately he did not ask us for insurance. Finally I looked at him and gestured that I would look out in future, and pointed to the Deafblind Scotland sticker on Wilson's top case. Unexpectedly, he decided to usher us off. I thanked him and could feel the relief coursing through my veins as we moved off again.

The road to David was in terrible condition and as the temperature hit 38C, it was not a good ride. Once in David we searched for a hostel that we had looked up the night before. It turned out to be closed, and we ended up going to the Bambu hostel which was really good despite ending up in a dorm with three other people. It had a pool, and $1 beers both a great relief in the heat. We chatted to a young Scottish girl from Perth who was having her own adventure travelling around by bus.

Costa Rica

Route Map

Tues 14/4/15

This was do or die day as far as getting out of Panama was concerned and I felt very tense. We had a 40-minute ride to the border, on straight and fairly clear roads. The first hurdle was a police and customs check just before the border. I forced myself to drop the worried approach and try a friendlier, outgoing one, more like I had been in the past. Next up was the Panama side of the border itself. There was an official helper there who guided us through the process. First the bike documents and passport stamps at immigration. I swallowed hard as they typed my details into the system, feeling a bit like that guy in the movie Midnight Express. No need, as next we went to customs, and then back to immigration without incident. The helper advised us that they would now check our bikes. As with the police stops, I was trying to hide my repairs in case these raised any questions. Fortunately they then decided not to check the bikes, and we were directed to go. The Costa Rica side was a little harder, with immigration first, then customs, then the insurance shop, then the photocopy shop, then customs, then a number plate check, then

FREEDOM! I was elated as I rode into a very green, tropical and pleasant looking Costa Rica.

The ride to Jaco was about 150 miles through pleasant, hot, lush countryside. Jaco is a surf town and the Room2Board Hostel was nice, and set close to the beach. It was owned and managed by a cocky American who reminded me a little of Bruce Willis. I indulged in the happy hour Caprianha cocktails that night in celebration of leaving Panama.

Wed 15/4/15

I would probably have preferred to be heading north but I was out-voted, and besides we did have time on our schedule, so we decided to have another night in Jaco. It was a lazy day, spent walking into town, writing, and doing a nuts and bolts check on Boris. The check revealed a missing nut on the top case support and some loose nuts on the pannier supports. It's a tedious job, but an essential one. The town itself had one major tourist street set back from the beach with lots of gift shops, bars and restaurants catering for the US tourists. I had a great encounter with an Armadillo who was simply wandering down the street.

"Natural hydration"

Thu 16/4/15

The ride north from Jaco brought some lovely coastal scenery, with many new resorts popping up. Our destination was Liberia, which was close enough to the Nicaraguan border for us to make an early crossing. The Hostel Dodera was available, and worked out well. It was run by an older American guy and his Costa Rican partner. It was small but perfectly formed, with an enclosed back garden laid out nicely with tables and chairs. Our hosts advised us we needed to pay an exit fee for the border, which would be easier to do in town at the bank. So we walked into town and eventually found the right bank and paid our escape fee. We stopped off in a McDonalds on the way back for a coffee, and were amazed to see the young Mexican family who had been part of our travelling community on the ferry Express crossing in Columbia. A small world indeed.

Nicaragua

Route Map

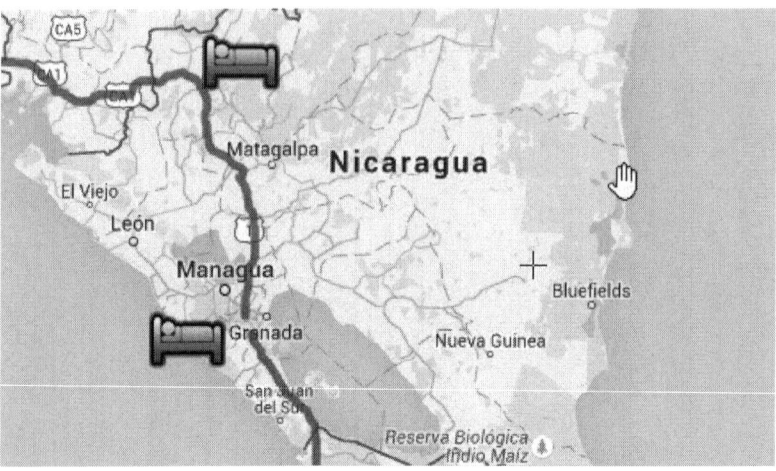

Fri 17/4/15

Our morning started with a great breakfast in a local cafe served by some cheerful women. From there it was a fairly straight and uneventful ride to the border. We had decided to go it alone i.e. no fixers, but as soon as we entered the area the fixers were on our case.

"No thanks" I barked at them.

We parked beside a cop, a tip picked up on the forums, and the fixers melted away. The Costa Rica side was pretty easy but the Nicaraguan side proved slightly tougher. The hardest bit was trying to get the main man to inspect our bikes. When we initially identified him he shrugged us off as he was busy with a bus. Remembering the rules of border crossings, we remained patient, though a little concerned. After around 15 minutes he indicated to us that he was ready. The process took minutes, then we had the stamp we needed. With immigration already complete, we had the customs woman process us, and we were done.

Nicaragua was a step down from Costa Rica in terms of western culture, but we liked the feel of it. The first part of the journey took us alongside Lake Nicaragua, which housed some extinct volcanoes. Unfortunately a heat haze dampened our view considerably. We then passed through the biggest and most ramshackle wind farm I have ever experienced, with various windmills missing blades or lying on their sides. Still, Nicaragua is trying to do their bit for planet saving. Our destination was Granada, which I had read about in previous travellers' accounts and which did not disappoint. It was a lovely city, very geared up for tourists, with good coffee shops, restaurants and bars. The hostel we had identified was full, so we managed to find a great value hotel that let us park the bikes in their lounge area. We had a good time that evening down on the Main Street, which is trying to be western, but thankfully and charmingly is not quite there yet. Putting the bikes in the dining area after a night out demanded revs and nerves and involved two steep ramps.

Sat 18/4/15

We backed the bikes out of the dining room with relative ease next morning, while the hotel owner watched Barcelona play Valencia on TV. I heard the familiar sound of GOOAAAAALLL Mesi!!!!! as I donned my bike gear in the already oppressive heat. The hotel owner gave us instructions on how to get quickly out of town, which worked a treat.

I was really enjoying Nicaragua with its pleasant green scenery, good roads and friendly people. The scenery got even more pleasant after we had skirted past the capital Managua and entered a tobacco growing area with lush meadows and small mountains.

"Tobacco plantation in Nicaragua"

The border destination of Somoto was perfect. Small and friendly, and the rooms were cheap enough at the Hotel El Rosario to enable us to have one each. We got more friendly warnings about safety in Honduras and El Salvador from a guest. There was nothing we could do but be sensible and aware. Tomorrow we would head through Honduras and into El Salvador.

Honduras and El Salvador

Route Map

Sun 19/4/15

Breakfast at the Rosario was a treat. We were led by the host into the owner's living quarters, where granny sat watching the Sunday morning church service. It was a great setting to eat delicious food served by the friendly female owner, who was clearly intent on filling us up. We were all a bit apprehensive as we rode towards the Honduras border. What would the border crossing be like, what would the country be like? Could we do two Central America border crossings in one day? I had deliberately planned a Sunday morning crossing as I assumed the fixers and bandits would be in bed or church. However had I read only that morning that you should not cross them at weekends. Information overload.

The exit out of Nicaragua was painless, and the entry into Honduras was painless in effort but slightly costly in dollars ($40). There were a few fixers on each side, but nothing bad. The two Amigos took the chance to have their boots polished up, but I was on a budget, no clean boots for me. The ride through Honduras was problem free. We even stopped to take some pictures of a local football match. We did get pulled over by the cops, but they were genuine and friendly, looking only for a picture of them to be taken with our bikes. They advised us that there had been an accident further up the road, so we might face a delay. Fortunately there was no real delay, as we did not fancy queuing in the hot sun. We filed past the accident scene slowly, noticing it involved a motorcycle. Raymond spotted what he believed was a child's body under a blanket. It was a horrible thought that some poor parents had lost their child that day.

"Friendly Honduras cops"

The exit from Honduras and entry into El Salvador was again very straightforward and friendly. When I say straightforward all of these border crossings take a minimum of a couple of hours, and a lot of moving around, but still, in the end, straight forward on this occasion.

We had planned to meet German, whom we had met at the ferry departure point in Columbia. Raymond was in contact with him, and a venue had been agreed. Wilson had identified a hotel in San Miguel as a contingency, which in the end we took as it was getting late and we did not wish to ride at night. We would meet German the next morning. We dined in a modern café next to the hotel that night. I reflected on the advice we had been given in Patagonia that we would go hungry in Central America due to the low quality food. It did not feel like it to me that night.

Mon 20/4/15

It was a short ride to German's village of San Sebastian, where he was born and raised. German had given us no address.

"Just ride into the village" he said, "You'll find me".

The village was up a small road, off the beaten track, and sure enough there ahead of us was his bright orange Kawasaki, sitting outside a traditional looking terraced house. He welcomed us warmly and introduced us to Anna, his friend and the owner of the house. Anna, probably in her fifties, had a grown up son and daughter, and a little new-born grandson. The house was simple and welcoming. It had a big living room, a garden full of mango trees and an outside loo. German was proud of his village, and very keen to show us around.

The first stop was the primary school, where we chatted to the headmaster or 'director' as he is known, about how it operated. The kids played all around us, excited about the visit from the gringos. Next up we visited the park, which German and his generation had created. It was centre pieced with a beautiful old tree. On our way there he bought a pink milky drink from a woman in the street, and then handed each of us a small plastic bag full.

"Bite the corner off and enjoy" he said with his dazzling smile.

For German it was a treat, for me it was a sickly endurance test which I had to get finished as soon as possible.

He then took us on a long walk into the countryside, teaching us how to tell if a mango was fresh and then showing us some natural springs he used to visit as a boy. As we walked we learned a little more about the man and the place. German was very active in the protests against the military regime in the seventies, and eventually had to flee the country into Mexico, and finally to the US where he now lives. He was apparently number three on a death list for the area, as he was head of propaganda. He initially settled in Mexico, then was smuggled over the border and deported several times over several years. Thankfully he made sure he was deported to Mexico, and not El Salvador. When captured the US guards told them to stand in two groups. Mexicans here and others over there.

"As far as they were concerned we all looked Mexican" he said with a smile.

"German"

He took us to the village cemetery, which was located at the top of a steep hill. He told us that the solders would come and rape the women and pillage the village. Anna's ninety-two-year-old grandfather was lined up and shot in her back yard, and he showed us the grave of a cousin who was raped and killed.

When we returned from our walk Anna had prepared a traditional lunch of chicken soup, followed by roast chicken cooked on an open fire. It was delicious, but made us all sweat even more in the sweltering heat. After lunch we went to visit the Mayor, who was a very friendly man in his thirties. He gave us a town mug, which I will always treasure. On the way out of town we stopped at a sugar beet processing plant. It was very traditional, and the end result is a substance that tastes very much like tablet but is all natural.

Later that afternoon we rode to German's cousin, Alexandra's house. She was not in, but he insisted we come to her cheese stall in the local market. German warned us that Alexandra is a larger than life character, and that was exactly how she turned out to be. The cheese stall was in a newly constructed, tin roofed market place. Alexandra had just moved there after spending fifty years in a traditional street stall. She sells five varieties of local cheese and operates from 6am to 5pm, 7 days per week. She is a 71-year-old matriarch and truly the queen of cheese. I loved her. As German had pre-warned us there was a constant flow of water, coffee, cheese and cake coming our way until we had to beg her, "No more".

"Alexandra - our El Salvadorian mum"

We went back to her house that night to wait for her son, who would be our host for the evening. She could not speak a word of English but kept us entertained nevertheless. Finally, two hours later than planned, Jorge rolled up and took us to his house, where we met his wife and thirteen-year-old son who reminded me of Manny in *Modern Family*. We bought beer, then Jorges's wife and 'Manny' were ordered to leave, while we had a 'man's night' on the rooftop terrace. As our room had only two beds, Wilson decided to sleep under the stars in the hammock. It turned out to be a bad decision as Jorge's assurances that there were no mosquitos were far from accurate.

It had been a very real and good day.

Tues 21/4/15

You can always be sure of one thing with German, plans change. We had been heading straight to San Salvador but now we had to go back to the market to say our goodbyes to Alexandra and her team. Goodbye consisted of three hours of sitting around at the stall. I used the time to get an El Salvadorian haircut, fortunately not by the barber who slit a former president's throat. Again plans changed, as seven of us piled into a five seat car to go for a late lunch, then a visit to a hot spring in San Vicente where the fish nibble at your feet like the ones in the malls in the UK. It was a great experience.

We finally did set of for San Salvador, unfortunately too late to get parts for my bike. We were to stay that night at German's nephew Mario's house. The house was small and very 'bachelor pad' like. In fact it was more workshop than house, but great. My bed for the evening was a couch. Mario is a charming young man who works in construction, while studying Architecture. His brother Gerson is also a great lad who is almost through a Law degree, but has a passion for cooking. We had an invite from the San Salvador BMW club, but opted to go out with the two boys instead. German took as to a fuel station supermarket while we waited for the lads to finish their classes. The walk was a bit like going through a war zone, and crossing the street was a nightmare.

"Why don't we cross at the lights?" I asked German "No point, nobody obeys them man" was the reply.

The lads came by just after 8pm, and the four of us climbed into the open back of their pick-up truck. This was another first for me as we whizzed through night time San Salvador. Raymond asked if I thought this was more dangerous than riding without a helmet.

"Absolutely" was my reply.

Nevertheless, like a lot of dangerous activities, it was great fun. We ate in a very traditional restaurant that night, up high on the hill, with great views over the city. On the way back German pointed to a square where his friends had been shot at a rally and told us how he had run for his life. This was a special night, never to be forgotten.

Guatemala

Route Map

Wed 22/4/15

We said our goodbyes and thanks to German as he left at 7am to meet an old friend. Gerson had invited us to his place for breakfast, then Mario would lead us to the edge of the city. I was regretting agreeing to this as I rode through the traffic, but then felt glad I did. Gerson served us a delicious eggs, refried beans and tortillas breakfast to die for. That boy should forget law and follow his passion.

Mario led us out of town and waved goodbye. The whole family had welcomed us into their homes and it had been a true pleasure to meet them all.

The ride to the border was short and the border crossing was very straight forward. Before we knew it we were in country number six, Guatemala. It was very like El Salvador both in scenery and in general conditions. We had our sights set on a hotel in Antigua which was a town recommend to us by some Mexicans we met at a border and also by German. The route to get there took us through Guatemala City which was busy but manageable. Antigua is set high in the mountains, surrounded by even higher volcanos. As we climbed towards the city the drop in temperature was like a breath of fresh air. The city itself was very old and had cobbled streets, old churches and cathedrals. It was a tourist town but we loved it. The hotel was fantastic and a reasonable price for a three bedded room. We had a good night that night, dining in an Italian restaurant.

"Fantastic hotel in Antigiua

Mexico

Route Maps

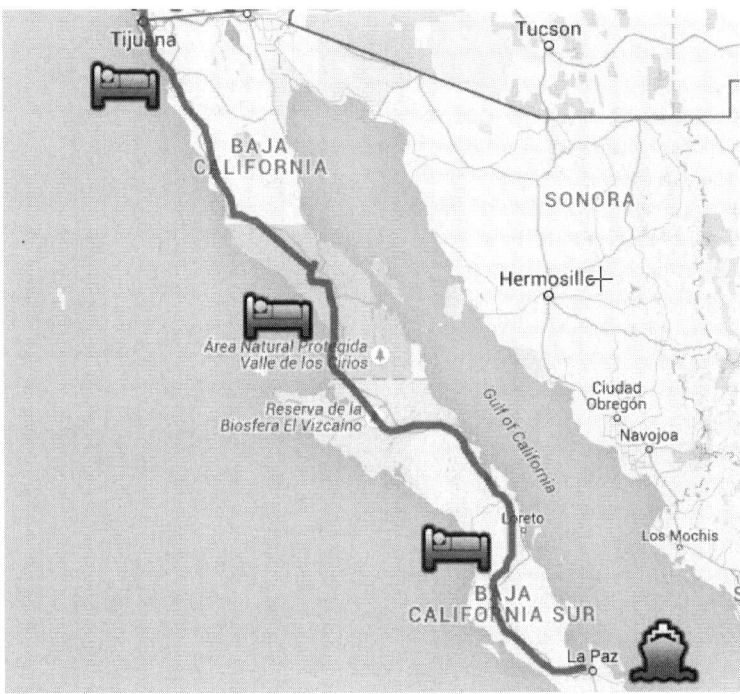

Thu 23/4/15

It was a long and hot ride to the Mexican border, made more bearable by an air conditioned stop at a Burger King in Escuintla. We were trying to find the quieter border crossing recommended to us by German, but roadworks and diversions were confusing us. A serious rain storm hit us just before the border, and I struggled to see through my steamed up visor. I had to resort to riding with my visor up which was incredibly uncomfortable. Still I was better off than the poor lady who had apparently just acquired a new mattress for her bed, and which was being soaked along with her in the back of a pick-up truck.

We did finally find the border and it was modern, efficient and easy on both sides. An official on the Mexican side advised us that we needed to go to a town some 70 kilometres north to acquire travel permits, but we could do it in the morning. He advised us to stay in a town called Tapachulaw that night, which sounded good to us. The short ride to Tapachulaw was great with a wide dual carriageway and modern infrastructure. We found a decent hotel for a decent price, and ate wonderful Mexican food al fresco on the square that night.

Fri 24/4/15

First priority next morning was finding the customs office to pay our permits. This was not straightforward, but could have been if we had not left the main highway. We finally found the place just north of town. The permit requires you to pay $400 to the Mexican authorities which they repay you on exit. It's like a ransom to make sure you don't sell your bike. The girl processed us fairly quickly and we were on our way.

Our next stop in Mexico was a town named Arriaga. Again the roads were great and we made good progress. I smiled as an old Volkswagen Beetle passed us with its rear air cooled engine cover open to help stop it over heating. There are lots of Beetles in Mexico as they continued to produce them there up until 2003. The town itself was fine, but the hostel we had identified turned out to be full. The receptionist recommended a couple of others and we chose the closest. It was basic, but the price was right and it had parking. As we parked our bikes the owner made the fatal mistake of ordering us to squeeze them into a corner with uneven ground in the empty lot. We protested, he insisted, so we left.

We went around the corner and found a better hostel where we could afford a room each. We were directed to the parking by a young boy, who gleefully rode pillion with Raymond. As we circled the block I had the horrible thought that we were heading for the car park we had just left. Thankfully it was another one located right across the street. We wandered about the town that night, at one point Wilson and I had to shrug off a drunk who wanted to be our best friend. We were enjoying Mexico.

"A Mexican Chihuahua"

Sat 25/4/15

German had raved about a town named Oaxaca when he was giving us advice for our route north and we were all looking forward to it. The ride was once again on excellent roads over mountain passes. Wilson was out in front while Raymond and I rode together for a while. Eventually Raymond stopped to take photographs, while I continued ahead alone. I am sure we all enjoyed the freedom of being on our own for a time. My only concern was that I was the only one without a working Sat nav or map, so I was relying on finding them again at some later point. I stopped off at a junction some ten miles out of the city, and waited for Raymond. It's times like that when you do consider the possibility that he may have fallen off and be lying somewhere down a slope. Thankfully the headlights appeared in the distance and we were reunited for the ride towards our target hotel in Oaxaca.

The city was big and it took a bit of time to get through the suburbs and into the old town. We spotted Wilson, who had been there for some time and had done all of the groundwork on hotels. The one we had identified was expensive, there was a cheap option (targeted at me) and a middle ground option. We decided to go for the middle ground option, and as they had no triple rooms Raymond and I shared while Wilson had the joy of his own room. I took a walk around and while it was a nice enough city with a big plaza hosting some kind of peaceful protest and market, it was nothing special. This was backed up by my two amigos who were also feeling a bit disappointed. The most disappointing aspect of the visit was the tourist-focused, overpriced, poor quality meal we had in the square that night. This added to a general bad feeling amongst us that evening.

Sun 26/4/15

The sun was shining the next morning and the new dawn had lifted our spirits. We walked towards the square looking for breakfast, but found only tourist options. Just as we were about to give up we spotted a restaurant that was in the process of opening. It was a great choice, and set us up for what would be a long day in the saddle. Today we would circle the infamous Mexico City. We had decided we would use the expensive toll roads to ensure we made good progress.

The roads turned out to be fantastic and we were amazed by how courteous the Mexican drivers were, often pulling onto the hard shoulder to let us pass. We crossed deserts and mountain ranges, gradually edging towards Mexico City. Thankfully Mexico had some great coffee shops at its fuel stations, with air conditioning to help keep us alert and refreshed. We hit some heavy traffic towards Mexico City, but the road quickly veered off and we circumnavigated the city by staying out in the quiet rural areas. We reached the exit to our target destination of Morelia, but found it was twenty plus miles off our route. After such a long day, and having ridden over 400 miles we had no appetite for a diversion.

The guys scrolled through the Sat nav ahead and found one hotel some fifty or so miles up the road. There was nothing before and very little after. We decided to go for it hoping we would make it before dark. La Posada Panindicuaro was a small hostel with gated parking and cheap enough to allow us to have a room each.

Panindicuaro was a very small town with a few very traditional cafés/restaurants on the small town square. The square was buzzing that night as we sat on plastic chairs enjoying some fantastic burritos cooked beside us in the open. Cars hooted their horns as they moved in procession around the square while kids jumped around on a bouncy castle. A burly guy wearing a gold chain and a white Cowboy hat entered the café to pick up some beer. He had an air of authority and power which we thought might be due to some kind of high status linked to criminal activity. He looked at us for a long minute, then ordered the waitress to get us a round of drinks. I am sure there was an element of showing off, but we appreciated the gesture. It was a good night.

Mon 27/4/15

I felt a gloominess hang over me like a thick cloud next morning. I was not sure if I actually felt physically bad too or whether it was all in my mind. I think it was mainly that I was peopled out and desperately needing a break. I think the crash and the after effects in Panama may also have played a part. That morning I yearned for the weeks break in LA. It was mid-morning and a large coffee later before I finally started to feel better, but I was not fully at my best all day. The ride was 400 miles plus again and the scenery was initially spectacular volcanic rock followed by fertile farmland. The ride was initially at a high altitude, but quite quickly dropped to sea level, and intense heat. We were resting in the shade of a garage when a man approached us. His name was Alex and he was a dentist in Mazatlán. He rode a GS800 and was keen to hear about our trip. Alex recommended the La Siesta Hotel which he said had a good location, was reasonably priced and that we could ride our bikes into the patio.

Alex told us he might call in and see us the next day. We finally arrived in Mazatlán early evening, and quickly found the hotel. It was actually on the beach, and at under £10 a head it was perfect. We ate in a nice restaurant that evening in a little square where the quality jazz trio next to us competed with some crazy brass band in the square. The crazy brass band silenced the quality trio.

Tues 28/4/15

I was so glad that we had put in the miles over the last couple of days thus earning a free day. We had a recommendation for the Panama restaurant for breakfast which was on the way to the Baja Ferry office, according to their website and Google maps. Despite not being fond of the name Panama, the restaurant turned out to be excellent. I had a dish named divorced eggs which was one egg covered in green Chile and the other in red Chile; it was delicious.

We then headed to the Baja Ferry office only to discover it was not where google said it was, but about a mile further on. I was delighted to learn our tickets would only cost about £80 each, including dinner and breakfast. Sadly for Raymond there were no cabins left, so we would have to rough it in a Pullman seat.

My next task was to arrange an oil change for Boris. I had considered doing it in the hotel courtyard, but my amigos had wisely talked me out of it. I decided I would ride around town looking for a Moto or Auto lube station, which are common in Latin America. I rode down one street enjoying the warm sunshine in my shorts and t-shirt until I eventually spied a bunch of motorcycles outside a small shop. I went in and tried to explain that I wanted to use their facilities to change my oil. With no common language they took that as "I need an oil change", and squeezed the bike into what seemed an impossible space, and began to work on it. Initially I was worrying about torque settings etc. but it soon became clear to me that this man knew what he was doing. I had a great time with the staff and the mechanic while the work was carried out. They seemed to enjoy the loco gringo and his big bike who were going to Alaska. In the end it cost around £20, including the oil, which was a total bargain.

I was smiling and satisfied as I rode Boris back to the hotel. After that it was Stevie time, spent doing some walking, internet and coffee drinking. That night we met Alex the dentist who had recommended the hotel, and his Canadian friend Brian. I am amazed at the number of Canadians who have colonized Latin America. Mazatlán had pleasantly surprised me. It had been a good productive and restful day.

"A Mexican oil change"

Wed 29/4/15

Today was another major milestone on our trip. Leaving the landmass of Mexico and heading towards the Baja Californian peninsula. It felt that I was now well on my way to meeting Amber in LA. The morning passed quickly as we sorted out potential accommodation, US Insurance and the like. As usual nothing was straight forward as I struggled to use a computer with a keyboard with worn out characters to print out an insurance form. Why they would not let me just email it to reception I will never know. I then had to beg a travel agency to scan a copy for me at a cost of 30 pesos. This was met by an out of office mail from the insurance agent.

Before I knew it, it was time to take the short ride to the ferry port. I led the way through the narrow streets and down to the ferry. The entry process was easy and we parked our bikes up in the hot sun. As with most ferries there were some other bikers waiting. One was Jim from England, who was traveling on a GS Adventure with his wife Jenny as pillion. Jim was ex-army and they had done much the same route as us, but at a more leisurely pace. They had been on the road for six months and expected to travel for another three months up to Alaska. They admitted they were Latin America'd out and looking forward to the US.

As with all Latin American schedules, things began to slip. First of all the ferry was not in port and there was no sign of movement. The sun was baking hot and there was little shelter, so it was not a pleasant experience. Eventually the ferry came in. It was old and rusty and looked like it had lost some of its upper deck, it had a strange shape. It seemed to take an age to disembark what seemed to be an endless stream of trucks. We must have waited for about four hours before we were finally called forward. When we did board we were sent up to the top of the ship, and placed next to a railing. There was no one there to help strap the bikes down, and initially there were no straps. I took some of my Rok straps off my Rotopax fuel carriers and used them to secure the bike. Eventually we did get some straps, but not enough. I hoped the sailing would be smooth, and Boris would remain upright. The ferry was very much geared up for trucks and drivers, with only basic facilities. Fortunately we had a bank of three Pullman seats on their own, but unfortunately we were surrounded by kids and babies. Could be a long night I thought to myself.

Dinner was basic but good, and as I settled into my seat I realized they had cranked up the air conditioning. While the others had fleeces and Raymond also had his bike jacket I was in a t-shirt. What could have been a decent sleep turned out to be a nightmare, as I fought off the chill air. I did get a few hours initially, but by 1:30am I got up looking for warmth. I tried all sorts of solutions, like going up on deck, but the wind created a cold chill there too. I then ended up lying comfortably on the floor down below, but was soon moved by the crew. In the end I had to just bear with it until the coffee place opened at 7am.

Thu 30/4/15

I wandered up onto the top deck to catch a little warmth from the rising sun. There were a few guys up there drinking beers. I hoped that they were not truck drivers that I might encounter on the road north. Wilson had befriended a cheerful Mexican guy named Victor Castillo who was on his way back with his fellow biker friend to a resort he worked at on the Baja. We were just off the coast of the Baja peninsula, which looked good in the morning sun with low hills and sandy coves. Breakfast was served at 9am, basic but delicious. We were told the ferry was now scheduled to arrive at 3pm, which seemed a long time coming. We finally docked at around 4pm and we were on the road north soon after.

La Paz looked like great town, very polished and attractive. We passed a beer café which was very very tempting in the heat, but we had to make some miles. We pulled over and ate at a local stall 50 or so miles up the road. The lady was smiling and friendly and made the most delicious shredded beef wrapped in a corn tortilla. "Mass?" she said "Si" we all replied. I stood behind the counter with her and her daughter to get our photo taken while her surly husband looked on.

"Fantastic roadside café in Baja, Mexico"

We entered the town of Villa Morelos where we pulled over into what looked like a new motel. They could only offer rooms with double beds, but at 500 pesos each we could afford our own space. Each room came with a garage, with an automated door. It was of a very high standard for the price. One of the boys noticed you could rent the rooms for three hours. I guess they may have been targeting several different markets?

We bought food at a supermarket just along the street and ate cheap that night.

Fri 1/5/15

The ride the next day was amazing, spoilt only a little by my frustration about team dynamics. There were amazing twisties and gorgeous sea views. We stopped off at one deserted beach and sipped water, gazing at the turquoise ocean lapping the white sands. Brunch was at a little restaurant where a Chihuahua nervously watched me eat my delicious Hevos Rancheros. Guerrero Negro, our chosen destination for that evening, was an unattractive little town set on the Pacific side. We rode separately for a while, meeting up at a fuel station in the middle of town. Raymond had identified a potential hotel on his way into town. It worked well as it was reasonably priced, and had a restaurant. We wandered along to the restaurant, but discovered it was closed for half an hour or so to clean up. Apparently today was "children's day" and they had just hosted an event. We ended up getting a great meal at a local restaurant located further along the street. It was run by a guy acting as the waiter with his wife doing the cooking and kids making noise and watching a cartoon. I guess they were entitled to do it as it was "Children's day". Wilson was, unusually, the sensible one that night, heading off as Raymond and I overdid it with the Tequila.

Sat 2/5/15

Next day's riding was less attractive in the main. We did have another great breakfast stop, where we met a bunch of Baja 1000 competitors from Arizona. The guys were just returning from a local race and chatted away to us for ages. Further up the road we pulled over onto the desert to get some photos of the bikes beside a cactus. We were only a few hundred yards from the road, but it felt as if we could have been in the middle of nowhere. Just up the road we managed to avoid a snake as it slithered across the hot tarmac. We stopped off for fuel at a garage next to the famous Mama Espinoza's hotel, which is a check point for the Baja 1000. The fuel stop was filled with bikers who were on an organised tour. We had passed them earlier, slowly and courteously of course. We finally arrived that night in Ensenada which was another tourist town, but looked great. The Baja 1000 boys had recommended a Casino Hotel, which turned out to be full. To be honest none of us fancied it anyway. We then managed to get a good room in the Casa Del Sol Hotel, right in the middle of the action. My sacrifice for a cheap night was to sleep on the floor, but it was one worth making.

There was a big boxing match going on that night in Vegas between the American Floyd Mayweather and the Mexican Manny Pacquiao, and the town was absolutely buzzing. There were TV's showing the event in every bar, outside and inside. We wandered through all the excitement to a place called Hussings, which is reputedly the oldest Cantina in Mexico, and the birthplace of Margaritas. It was a great place with a great atmosphere, almost like a traditional Scottish pub. We watched the boxing while drinking our Margaritas and eating peanuts. As is the tradition, you just deposit the shells on the shell strewn floor. Felt a bit strange, but everybody was doing it. It made for an interesting noise when you were walking to the bar for a round. After the boxing (Manny was robbed) a traditional live band played amongst us. A great ending to a great night.

"Hussings Cantina"

USA

Route Maps

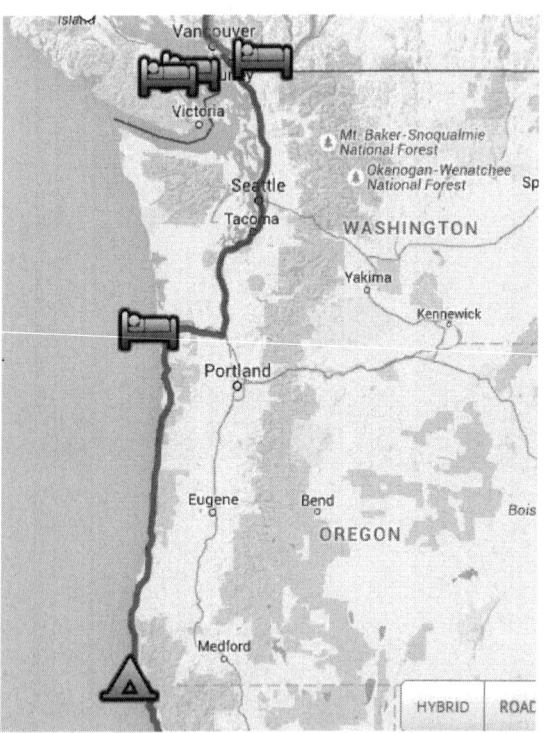

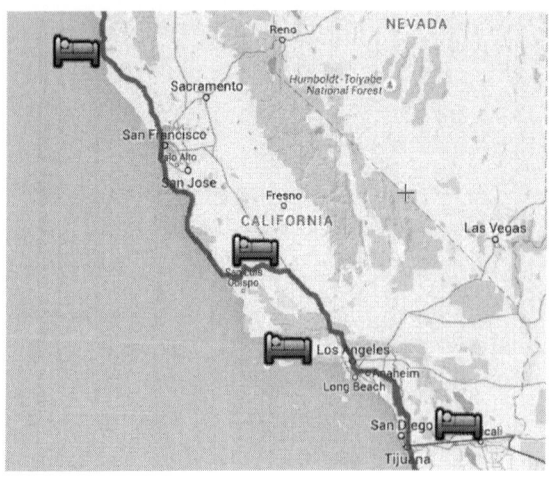

Sun 3/5/15

This morning would bring another major milestone, our departure from Latin America. It felt exciting but at the same time sad. We had a last Mexican breakfast in a local café that certainly did not let us down. We will all remember Mexican food with great fondness, especially the breakfasts. The ride north was on a dual carriageway cut into the cliffs directly above the coast. It was spectacular, and not what I had expected at all. My vision had been of busy, grubby and heavily populated towns from Ensenada to the border.

We finally entered the famous border town of Tijuana, where our first priority was to look for the place to reclaim the deposit for our vehicle passes. We had been instructed by the Baja 1000 riders to go to a border near the airport. As we searched around Raymond spotted an insurance office and suggested we go there. I was still feeling bad about the amount I had paid, so I selfishly and reluctantly agreed. I was not, however, keen to stand in the sun guarding the bikes as requested while they checked it out. It turned out to be closed.

We continued on our search for the deposit return office, and were directed up a nearby slip road by a grumpy cop. The slip road led us onto the queue for the border check, with no chance of return. My heart sank; I was sure we had missed our chance to get our money back.

Raymond and Wilson then found a guy who would sell them insurance for $107 which was nearly £200 cheaper than I had paid. They had liability only, while I had full comprehensive, but in all honesty I felt cheated. Raymond's confidence that there would be an opportunity to get our deposit back fell apart when after snaking through the traffic a nice young officer said "Welcome to the United States". The entry into the U.S. was so easy with a fee of $6. We asked about the Mexican ransom, and were advised that we would have to return to Mexico to get that.

We pulled up at a McDonalds to discuss our options. We decided we would park up our bikes at a cost of $7 each, and walk back in. Wilson did comment that they may need to see the bikes, but for some inexplicable reason we decided to ignore that. Fortunately the weather was a lot cooler now, but still hot enough to make us sweat as we made the long walk down the street and over the bridge. No one at the Mexican border was interested in us, and we were waved on. We showed our documents to a customs official, who gave us directions to the right office about half a mile away. They could not have placed this office in a more obscure location; I get the feeling the Mexican government make lots of money out of people who give up on this.

As you may have predicted they needed to see the bikes, and as it was a Sunday they closed at 4pm, just 40 minutes away. I suggested to Wilson we stay the night in the U.S, just over the border, and come back in the morning with the bikes. We headed back into the U.S and collected the bikes. Raymond had been told he needed a document to enable him to export his bike from the U.S, so we also decided to see if we could track down the issuing office. We finally found it, but it was closed. Luckily we met a super friendly officer who was leaving for home and who agreed that he would get the document there the next day. He also confirmed that Wilson and I did not need the document as we were shipping from Canada.

After sorting that out it was time to say adios to Raymond. He had a hotel booked in San Diego, and would head off on his own after that. His plan was now to ride into Alaska and take the inner passage ferry south to Seattle. From there he would take the tourist route back to LA. He would ship Sheila from LA to Oz. Wilson and I were heading for LA and a break with our wives. Hopefully we would meet somewhere further north for a night or two. As guys do, there was a quick handshake, an awkward hug and he was gone. I wondered how he would do on his own, confident he would be ok.

Wilson and I located a Holiday Inn Express less than a mile away and checked into that for the night.

And now there were two.

Mon 4/5/15

We decided to unpack our bikes and leave the bags with the hotel to make the entry check into Mexico easier and faster. The entry process turned out to be very easy, and before long we were processing our deposit return. We returned to the area where the queue for the US entry lined up. Wilson had checked his insurance document that morning, and discovered that it was valid for Mexican citizens only. He managed to track down the guy who sold it, and got a refund. We then proceeded through the border with relative ease, and back to the hotel. Wilson spent a long time trying different insurance options but in the end bought the same policy as I had. I felt better that I had not made a muck of the research on that.

We then headed into Long Beach on the fast, but relatively quiet, five lane highway. It felt weird, but good, to be back in the USA. Our first task was to locate Long Beach BMW, which turned out to be a very large and impressive shop. Richard, the guy I had been dealing with, greeted us warmly and went through the process of explaining what we needed. He pointed out that I needed a drive shaft gasket, which I had not spotted. I asked him to think creatively, not like a standard BMW dealer, when dealing with my bike, repair rather than replace. He got my meaning, and said he would do his best. In the end we agreed he would fit indicators, replace the rear tyre with a like for like Continental TCK70, fit the spark plugs that I had been carrying, and replace the drive shaft gasket. He said the headlight assembly would be too expensive, and potentially complicated due to the crash damage.

"Enjoying our Long Beach BMW experience"

Wilson and I then spent time in the showroom and accessories area which again was big and well stocked. A guy formally from Hungary took an interest in us and helped us book a hotel. He was nice but a bit over-communicative. Apparently he was a former maths professor now advising on the stock market. We also got talking to Luis Herrera, an architect, who was an active member of Piston and Chains, the super cool motorcycle club in San Francisco where you can work on your own bike.

We finally got a taxi out to the hotel, which was dated but adequate, and walked through a dubious area that night to get a cold beer and some food. It was definitely going to be a cab for the return journey. Strange that after all that time in the "dangerous" South, we were least at ease on our second night in the USA.

Tues 5/5/15

We had checked the night before and had discovered we could take a $70 taxi or a $3.50 metro to the airport. Despite the bags and bike gear the Metro won hands down. The ride was straight forward with one change in between, and a bus at the end. I commented on how I had seen more mentally ill looking people in a few hours in LA than in the whole of Latin America.

At LAX (LA Airport) we took the Dollar Hire Car bus out to the depot and picked up our cars. Thankfully it was not too busy so the process was very smooth for me. Wilson had an issue using a pre-paid credit card and had to hunt me down in the car park for assistance. We were finally sorted and ready to go. I laughed as I followed Wilsons 4x4, dwarfing my wee Mitsubishi, still he had more driving to do than me. We drove back into the short stay car park in LAX and headed across to arrivals to patiently await our loved ones.

5/5/15 – 12/5/15

Our time and a chance meeting with Raymond at the BMW dealer as he set off north. Ride safe Amigo.

Tues 12/5/15

After saying goodbye to Amber and Yvonne we returned to Long Beach BMW to pick up the bikes. We had a good chat with Richard the service manager and a local cop who was in getting his Police Bike repaired. Richard described Highway 1 north of San Francisco as "bitching". The solemn cop smiled when asked if that meant it was a good road or a bad road. We had planned to just blast up Highway 5 to San Francisco but the cop talked us into taking the exit at Lost Hills, and heading to the coast.

The ride out of LA was busy but manageable, fairly straight forward with the exception of one wrong turn followed instantly by another, which we then had to quickly correct. We crossed some mountains before finally levelling off on the Central Californian plains. The land was flat and fertile but not particularly interesting. That cop was right with his advice. We stopped at Lost Hills for fuel then made our way to our stopover destination of Paso Robles. We first tried a Best Western but that was expensive, so we asked the receptionist if she knew anywhere cheaper. She kindly sent us to the Motel 6, which was just perfect, with a little local Mexican Restaurant right next door.

On first approach the restaurant looked closed, but thankfully it was just quiet. It served good food and draft Dos Equis Amber beer, what a great result. It had felt great to be back on the bikes again and after a late start we had made significant progress already that day. As we walked back to the hotel, I noticed there was a dramatic drop in temperature based on what we had been used to, but I preferred it.

Wed 13/5/15

We had a short ride next morning to join Pacific Highway 1 at San Simon. On the way I noticed my headlight dipped beam was not working. I winced at the thought of having yet another bike problem to deal with. I guess it would be a bulb, but what kind? It was HID and not the standard. I guess I would have to rely on my old friend, the internet, to work it out.

From San Simon we were retracing the route from our trip the previous year, heading due north. That time I was on a hired BMW 1600, this time my very own Boris. We had left before 7am and the road was fantastically quiet and as is described by many, an awesome road. We decided to do some Go-Pro filming that morning and pulled over a few times to switch the cameras on and off. It was at one of those stops my headlight started working again and did so for the remainder of the trip. I was chuffed.

My Panamanian repair to my broken speedometer glass (a Tupperware lid) had one little flaw. It was not opaque enough to see through. This had not been an issue in the less speed limit conscious south but we knew from experience that speeding in the USA did not make sense. I had warned Wilson that I was relying on him to keep us legal. I must admit I was enjoying the ride up Highway 1 thinking to myself 55mph is actually a nice pace. It was only when we encountered one of those speed display boards that I realized Wilson was not sticking to the plan. "Hey you bugger were doing 75" I yelled across the Scala. "Really" came the reply. No wonder we made such good progress.

Eventually we stopped off at the Nepenthe Restaurant and Café at Big Sur for breakfast with a view over the ocean. Wilson had found this place on a previous trip. Located high up on a cliff Nepenthe was once owned by Orson Welles and Rita Hayworth. It was an idyllic breakfast in an idyllic spot with brightly coloured birds perching beside us, watching as we ate. From there we rode up past Carmel, Monterey and Santa Cruz and on into San Francisco. Before long we were crossing the Golden Gate Bridge where we stopped off for a photo of us proudly holding our Deafblind Scotland banner.

"Raising the standard at the Golden Gate Bridge"

From there we headed on up Highway 101, then cut over to a quaint little town called Bodega Bay, soon re-joining Highway 1. The road from Bodega Bay up to Fort Bragg was indeed "bitching". Just before reaching Fort Bragg Wilson had stumbled upon a little Motorcycle shop in Point Arena called The Zen House. We nearly missed an opportunity to visit there, because, true to form, I did not see Wilson or the shop and rode right by. He had to ride fast to catch me and to make sure we were back before closing. The shop is run by David and Trash (yes she confirmed that was her name). David used to run a Ducati dealership in San Diego and had done a round the world trip lasting over a year and a half. He had an amazing collection of bikes, mainly old Ducati's. We spent a great half hour with him in his Aladdin's Cave of a shop. What a find.

We finally arrived at Fort Bragg which was a typical small American town, checked into a motel on Main Street and used its adjacent restaurant.

Thu 14/5/15

The weather was pretty damp looking next morning as we set off, but turned out fine. We had discussed the possibility of riding to Crater Lake, which is reputed to be beautiful and was where Wilson had also spoken about hooking up with an old colleague. We pondered over the map and routes for some time and in the end decided to stick to the coast. The route north was stunning, coast followed by an amazing forested mountain crossing taking us right into the Redwoods and Big Foot country. We stopped off at the Chandelier, a drive through tree, to get some photos as Raymond had some days before. We then took a scenic route called "The Avenue of the Giants" which was just amazing, with the sun dappling the road through the trees. We stopped a few times just to soak in the calm of the atmosphere.

As we approached the Oregon border we stopped off at a liqueur store that was making great claims about its value for money. "The liqueur is cheaper in California" they said as we picked up some wine. It turned out not to be true, but the stop was worth it, as the heavily tattooed woman serving there pointed us to what was a stunning campsite. Harris Beach State Campsite in Brookings, Oregon, is located in the trees beside a fantastic beach with tall, narrow, rocky islands just off shore. It was a magnificent return to camping, with a fire pit and bench at each plot. We pitched up, then rode into town to Fred Myers, a large supermarket chain, for supplies. We had a great night by the fire eating pre-packed salad and boiled eggs, delighted to be camping again.

Fri 15/5/15

The weather was once again damp looking next morning as we set off. It turned out to be the equivalent of a poor Scottish summer's day with intermittent downpours! We made an early stop at a local restaurant called Double D's in Gold Beach, where we had a great laugh with the locals and the mature waitresses - mainly at our expense.

The route north was stunning in places, and ordinary in others as we were often out of sight of the coast. I noticed sign-posts for the Lewis and Clarke museum and deduced this must have been the area where they reached the Pacific coast some 210 years before us. Now those guys were real hard core adventurers.

We rode into Astoria passing beneath a massive bridge. There were a number of hotels and motels on the outskirts of town, but we decided to check the centre first. After a quick whiz around the one-way system we headed back out to a place we spotted earlier, the Astoria Lamplighter Motel. The Motel itself was great, but our stay was wasted by some idiots who decided to party all night in the room above us.

Canada

Route maps

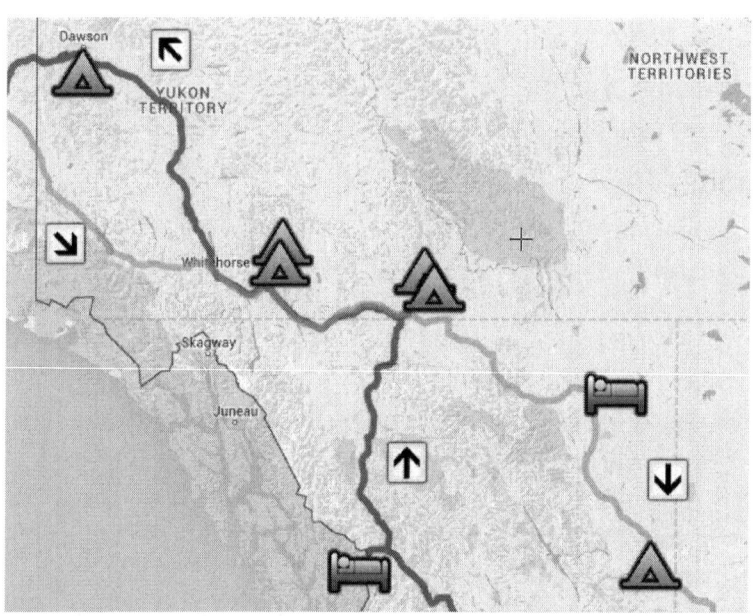

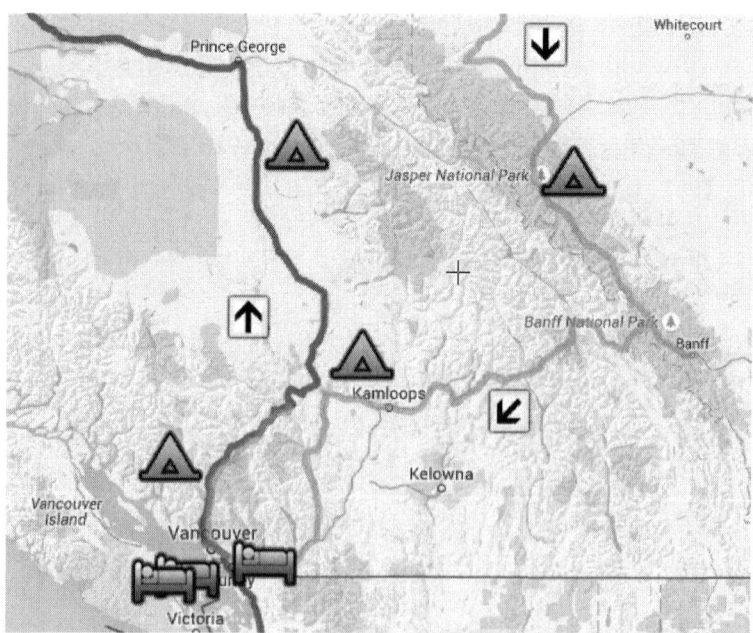

Sat 16/5/15

Another wet start next morning, but a fairly pleasant ride. We eventually picked up highway 5, routing us efficiently through some bland countryside towards Seattle.

I was thinking about the fact we were probably only two or three days behind Raymond now having originally been six. As I watched Wilson making good pace up front with me tucked in behind, I had a vision of the Orcs chasing the Hobbit in Lord of the Rings.

The city itself was easy to ride into, and just like Glasgow, the freeway routed right through the centre. Downtown Seattle looked more compact than I had anticipated, but impressive with its skyscrapers all huddled together. I nearly had an incident due to me asking a Harley guy while riding if we could use the car pool lane. When I looked ahead the traffic had stopped and I had to swerve sharply to avoid it. Another close call.

We had hoped to visit the Touratech motorcycle accessory shop in Seattle, but were astounded to learn it did not open on a Saturday; I found that bizarre, surely that would be a peak time for bikers? We pulled off the highway for a coffee break, but had trouble finding a place in this city, famously the home of Starbucks. We finally found a fuel station and a McDonalds which satisfied our need for the time being.

There was some further bland highway riding north from Seattle, but we could now see the mountains of Canada in the distance. We arrived at a polished and efficient border crossing and in no time at all we were in our final, fifteenth, country. At last I could say that I had earned all of my small country flag stickers, which I had attached to Boris like a pilot attaching kill stickers to his Spitfire; it felt good.

Canada was sunny and bright, and the ride through Vancouver was manageable, but busy. Again I am pretty sure the Sat Nav did not take us by the most efficient route, but we eventually did pop out the other side of the city, and we were in for a treat. The route north towards Whistler was spectacular, with the highway snaking high on the hillside, looking over a glistening coast with Vancouver Island in sight.

We pulled over at a nice looking town called Squamish, where there was a Supermarket and a Camping shop next door to each other, meeting all of our needs. We enquired about campsites independently, providing us with a couple options. Wilson's option of Alice Lake, located just up the road seemed like the best option. Mine was closer to Whistler, more obscure, and the guy who advised me said it was a holiday weekend, that we might be lucky and find a space there. It turned out that Alice Lake was indeed full so we continued on towards Whistler, to the Cal-Cheak Recreation Site across from the entrance to the Winter Olympics Park.

There were three loops, each with multiple pitches. The first and second loop were jam packed and the third, thankfully, had one space, or so we thought. Just as we were getting ready to unpack I noticed a sign saying that this pitch was closed due to dangerously weak trees. We were disappointed, and contemplating our next move when a young man in his late twenties came over and offered to let us share his spot. His name was Kevin Chow, and he was also riding a R1200GS, similar to Boris, but straight and unmarked. His two friends, Josh and Adam welcomed us warmly. Adam had a Scooby Doo style van while the other guys had one man tents.

In all honesty there was nowhere sensible to pitch our tents, but pitch them we did. I had a young sapling lifting up one side of my groundsheet by about a foot. Luckily with our experiences of camping in Argentina and Chile, it seemed fine. We had a wonderful night with the guys exchanging stories around the campfire. Kevin called his Aunt who lived further north and arranged for us to camp in her garden. This was just "awesome man" as Kevin himself would have said.

"Left to right Josh and Kevin"

Sun 17/5/15

The term 'recreation site' seemed to translate into very few facilities and they got even fewer when I discovered that the toilet was closed in the morning. Desperate times led to desperate measures, forcing me to find a remote spot in the woods. I recalled the 'Bear Warning' signs posted prominently around the campsite as I squatted nervously....

The others started to rise, and Kevin gave me a bolt from his bike to replace one that had shaken loose from mine. What a gem of a guy. We bade our friends farewell, and set off North, stopping at the famous Ski resort of Whistler to take a look around. It was nice, Alpine, fancy and expensive looking. We rode on, starting to scour for a breakfast option, with a toilet where we could get cleaned up. The breakfast option was tucked away in a little town called Pemberton, and it was perfect. '

Kevin had raved about the next part of Highway 99 which crossed a mountain range into Lillooet. Wilson headed off in front as we started the steep climb. It was quite cold and the roads were damp in places, but the sun was out. I was enjoying the ride with its twists and turns and undulations. The scenery was fantastic, with snow covered peaks sticking up from the forested mountains. There were fast flowing rivers, still lakes and very little traffic. I was delighted with our progress and feeling good as I approached a tight right hand bend and sailed around sweetly.

Just after the corner there was a bridge, which had a tight left hand bend coming off it. I noticed the bridge surface was made from wooden planks and closed off the throttle straight away. As soon as I hit the bridge the bike went into a slide, as if on an icy surface. I made a slight adjustment to take the corner and the bike instantly slid from beneath me. I got up straight away and ran towards the bike. My heart sank when I saw a pool of oil on the road just beneath it. I waved a guy in a pick-up truck down and asked him to help me lift it. We both heaved poor Boris upright, and I pushed him over to the side of the road. The guy offered me a lift, but also suggested that I could free wheel into Lillooet as it was downhill all the way. By that time a few other cars and a Harley had passed by peering to see what was going on. I thanked the guy and waved him off, then checked Boris for the source of the leak. At that point I was telling myself "your trip is over -it's all over". I realised I had a few bruises, but once again nothing major as I gingerly got onto the bike to freewheel into town.

The first kilometre or two I was able to freewheel, but as I passed a sign telling me I had 20 kilometres to go a steep climb loomed in front of me, and I realised the guy had got it badly wrong. My mind was in overdrive as I wondered what to do now. My bike has an oil warning light, and although there seemed a lot of oil on the road, I thought that maybe there was still just enough to ride on. I fired Boris up, and the warning light stayed off, so I pulled away riding slowly, killing the engine every time I hit a downhill section. I had visions of a crack in my engine block spewing oil, and I kept my hand on the clutch, ready to react to an engine seizure locking my rear wheel. It was not a comfortable ride. About 5 kilometres out of town Wilson rode towards me, and I gave him the thumbs up. A lady in a car and the Harley couple had seen him waiting for me at a gas station in Lillooet, and had stopped to tell him what was happening. They had said I looked all right but the bike didn't, and he knew he wasn't going to be sure until he found me.

We pulled over at a viewing point, and I told him I was fine but that Boris had a catastrophic oil leak. I told him about the bridge to which he replied

"I came so close to falling off there as well. I actually slid across it but managed to brake before hitting the verge without actually taking the corner".

That helped a little with the deep sense of shame and embarrassment that I felt for having had another off.

He was calm and suggested heading for the gas station to check things out. We made it to there, and checked Boris over. I had smashed an indicator again, but it was still working. Other than more wear on the crash bars the oil leak was our only real problem and we still could not see the source of it. We decided to top the oil up and ride into the small town centre, to see if we could find a garage. It took about two litres to top it up which, considering it holds four, was a significant amount. It was Sunday and it seemed unlikely that there would be any garages open in town. The gas attendant pointed us towards a couple, and also a car parts and accessories store.

We decided to try the parts and accessories store and, if it was open, we would strip down the bike outside and look for the leak. I had in mind that we could fix it with steel epoxy. Thankfully the shop was open, and they had several varieties of epoxy. We took off the crash protectors and looked for a sign of a leak, but could see no cracks. There was oil around the spark plug cap. Maybe it had just spilled out because of the impact, maybe we should try to just keep going. We set off north, out of town, then pulled over after a few miles to check.

"It's no good" said Wilson, "I can see oil dripping on the road".

My heart sank once again and, feeling low, rode back into town with my clutch hand at the ready. We returned to the store and got the name of a local recovery service. I explained my situation and felt like crying when they told me they would charge $800 to take the bike to BMW in Vancouver. We asked the store if there was a bike shop in town, but there was none.

"You could always try Bob" the guy said.

Bob was a retired motorcycle mechanic living in town. A customer said he would be passing Bob's house and would send him down. Meanwhile Wilson and I decided to try tightening the spark plug. The spark plug lead on my bike actually includes the coil, and it needs a special tool to remove it. Luckily Stevie the mechanic had made sure we left with one. The problem was neither Wilson nor I could quite remember how to use it. I took responsibility and gave it a yank which resulted in a cracking noise which resulted in instant despair. I had snapped it. Things were going from bad to worse. Bob did not show up, so Wilson got directions to his house and went looking for him.

After a lot of effort, he managed to track him down, and get him to come take a look. While Wilson was gone a chatty guy was doing my head in, constantly asking me questions. I was doing my best to be civil but in the end I explained I was not in a good place for a conversation. Wilson arrived followed by Bob on his cracking 1940's vintage Indian motorcycle. Bob was in his sixties and had a long grey beard. He exuded experience.

He took a look at the coil and said

"Can't fix it"

Then took a look at the oil leak and said

"It's your gasket".

He added

"You can ride it on one cylinder to Vancouver to get it fixed. It shouldn't leak much oil and you can always top it up".

"Really?" I asked, "are you sure?"

He turned the key and fired Boris into life.

"Go-ahead" he said.

We asked him if there were any good bike shops north of there that could possibly help. We already knew that the only BMW dealer heading north was some 1800 miles away in Fairbanks. He said the only possibility would be New Life Cycles.

 "That guy has everything".

I tried to pay him but he shrugged me off and waved as we shouted thanks.

"Bob to the rescue"

We had already agreed we would stay over in Lillooet that night, and make a move in the morning. We rode along the main street, and pulled into a reasonably priced motel. I still felt like shit about what had happened. I hated the thought of turning back and riding 200 miles south but was not convinced that I would be able to get it fixed up north. I told Wilson he should ride on regardless, but to his credit he said he was staying with me. He too must have been feeling frustrated by now. That night we went to the local hotel for dinner and were entertained by a high spirited cowgirl with her low key partner as they were out celebrating her birthday. After a few beers Wilson and I clinked our glasses and decided, lets ride north!

Mon 18/5/15

I awoke early the next morning, feeling anxious and wondering what to do. I gave myself a good talking to. There are three BMW dealers in greater Vancouver within 200 miles, there is a one bike salvage yard and no BMW dealer for 1800 miles. Ok, so we should head south. I had sent a mail the previous night to Dave at New Life Cycles, asking about the part, but as it was bank holiday Monday there had been no reply. I messaged Stevie in Parks Garage at home, for a second opinion on riding on one cylinder. No problem, he said, it's a twin spark. I remembered I had two spark plugs per cylinder so I guessed I would be riding on one and a half cylinders. Stevie also confirmed the oily spark plug outlet meant gasket. He advised that it's often just a clean-up that's required for a fix. I decided to have a go at removing and cleaning the gasket before we set off but couldn't completely remove it due to the crash bar. Then I struggled to put it back together, but thankfully Wilson managed to get it secured.

The climb south out of Lillooet is really steep so Boris would have an early endurance test. I had to stay down one or two gears lower than normal but we managed the challenge and kept going. We stopped off at the top of the mountain to check the oil, and all seemed to be holding well.

Wilson hung back and took more photos as I nursed Boris towards Vancouver. It was an uneasy ride, constantly watching the oil warning light and struggling to pass camper vans and the like. Eventually we rolled into Vancouver and headed for Vancouver BMW and Ducati just on the off chance that they would be open. Sadly they were not, so we found a local Hotel close by, ready for Tuesday morning. I patted Boris as I parked up thinking of how I have put him through the mill and he just keeps going.

Tues 19/5/15

I was anxious on waking, thinking about how things would go. Would they have the parts; would they have the time? Wilson seemed to be taking forever to get going, but I was aware he had done me a big favour coming back with me, so I decided to be patient. I am sure he sensed my agitation though. We arrived just as Vancouver BMW-Ducati opened and I was helped by Daniel, a confident young man. He checked for parts, and noted that he needed to get the coil stick, but that it should be available in Vancouver; he would get it delivered and send us on our way today. That was just what I needed to hear. Wilson enquired about a replacement front tyre, but they didn't have the right one in stock. Daniel called another dealer who did have the tyre, so we headed over there.

I rode pillion, and before long Ludwig was shod and we were on our way back. The parts had still not arrived so we took another trip to an outdoor store to pick up tent pegs for me and binoculars for Wilson. After that there was a lot of hanging around, considering we were in a motorcycle store this was not a great hardship. In fact at one point both of us fell fast asleep on the couches in the middle of the showroom. The staff quite rightly gave us a bit of a ribbing later. Finally just before closing at 6pm Daniel announced "We're done". The mechanic, Rory, was tattooed, had a Mohican haircut and was brilliant. He showed me that I had actually sheared my rocker cover, clearly amazed and amused at the level of damage done. Amazingly they had one in stock so it was fitted and ready to go. Not great for my wallet, but great to be once again mobile. I patted Boris as I left the dealers thinking, unstoppable indeed.

"Rory enjoying my unusual damage"

We headed out of Vancouver with no real traffic issues. Our target was the Alice Lake campsite just north of Squamish that had been recommended to Wilson last time around. We stopped off in Squamish for supplies then checked into the site. It was a cracking location in the woods, and was now very quiet. We sat by the fire enjoying the night sky and looking forward to heading north again.

Wed 20/5/15

It felt like dejavu that morning as we headed back up the Sea to Sky highway. We even planned to stop off for breakfast at the same place in Pemberton but it was closed. Instead the attendant at the gas station recommend a place next door which turned out to be a fantastic choice. Then we did the now familiar ride over the mountains, although this time I stayed upright. I was by now seriously over-cautious when it came to wooden bridges. I had been feeling angry with the Canadian government for setting up such a death trap of a surface for bikers, and convinced myself that the warning signage was poor. We stopped off at 'my bridge' and saw the "20km/h and Slippy" signs. It made me realise I had to take some accountability here too.

The road beyond Lillooet was a disappointment. I was hoping for more of the same but it turned out to be fairly flat and rural. We passed the quirkily named towns of 70 Mile House, 100 Mile House and 150 Mile House which was, of course, 50 miles north of 100-mile house. We passed through Williams Lake and decided to stop off at Dave's New Life Cycles. Whilst in Vancouver Dave had replied saying he did not have the part I needed so I had made the right decision back then. Dave's place was just out of town and off the highway. He was well into his sixties with blonde hair and a face which looked full of knowing. I think he did not quite know what to make of us at first, but he warmed to us after a short time, and shut up shop to take us on a tour of his premises. He had room after room jam packed with whole and stripped motorcycles of all ages, shapes and sizes except of course a R1200GS. Dave had done a couple of South American trips himself so we swapped stories for a while. He also gave me some rubber hose pipe to fix my loose Garmin bracket. We enjoyed this stop immensely.

We arrived early evening at our destination of Quesnel and blew our directions straight away as Walmart loomed before us. I had remembered Kevin saying, "If you reach Walmart you've gone too far". I took the opportunity to visit Walmart to replace my broken camera sim, then after a bit of faffing around we finally found Kevin's aunt's house on the lake.

Kevin's aunt, Signe, came out and greeted us like long lost sons and directed us to her junkyard back lot. Junkyard in a good way as it turned out, with her husband, Butch, having a passion for collecting things. There were a couple of old Suzuki Jeeps, a VW Camper, a boat and a flatbed trailer amongst others. Signe told us to pitch away from the lake as it could get windy during the night. She also advised if we needed to "dew the grass", to do it behind the Suzuki. For 'the other kind', she would leave the back door open. She looked at the sorry state of my twice crashed jacket and ordered me to hand it over.

"Are you hungry?" she asked with a knowing smile.

"Yes" we replied "but we can go get something".

"Don't be crazy" she said "I will cook you guys up some fish".

 As soon as we had the tents up she invited us into her home. Butch and their son Vahn, a college student, were there to welcome us. We were later joined by Kevin's cousin Ben, and Reg who is a friend of Butch. Signe signalled us over to pick up a plate full of delicious fish, potatoes and vegetables. It was a delicious meal and we had an amazing night with the family. Signe even sewed a patch on my jacket.

Thu 21/5/15

There was a lot of dew in the air as we packed up our tents next day. Signe came to say goodbye before heading off to work, soon followed by Butch, who hung around for a while to watch our progress. I gave Butch my Scotland flag as he had Scottish roots, just a small gesture, but I think he appreciated it. Then we set off, heading for a breakfast spot in town that had been recommended by Kevin. At this point we encountered one of the few pain in the arse people of the trip. A grumpy Harley rider moaning about our parking and our 5 yards ride up a one-way street.

Then Wilson thought he had forgotten his map heading back to Butch's, while I headed north towards Prince George. I made good progress so it was way beyond Prince George before he caught up with me again; I was stopped off at a gas station. I sensed he was by now in a "leave me alone mood" which I could relate to, and continued on while he fuelled up and hydrated. My next stop off was at a little tourist information office in Smithers where I picked up a brilliant free map for North West Canada and Alaska.

Finally we made the start of the 'Stewart Highway' and rode up to Meziadin junction where we enquired about camping or a motel; there was nothing suitable, so we decided to ride a one way, 40-mile detour to the town of Stewart itself. I was getting tired and frustrated about having to go in the wrong direction after such a long day, but was soon rewarded. I came round a bend and right by the side of the road was a huge grizzly bear. I instinctively braked, wheeled around and rode to within a couple of hundred yards of this magnificent creature. My heart was pounding as I fumbled and flapped, trying to get my camera out of my bike pocket. I had swung the bike around, pointing away from the bear, and left my engine running in case I had to make a run for it. I took several photos then rode off feeling elated by this close encounter.

"My first bear encounter"

It was a superb unplanned detour, with amazing scenery, including a glacier sinking right into the valley. Then I headed into town where Wilson was waiting to discuss accommodation. I pushed for a hotel option as I thought Wilson needed a good rest that night.

While there we received a message from Captain Jim, whom we had met on the Baja Ferry, to say the Dalton Highway, our final highway in Alaska was closed due to flooding. This was a major blow but when we checked the website it said they expected it to reopen on Friday 29/5, one week from now. We could work around that.

Fri 22/5/15

"Did you have your snozzle in?" was my morning greeting. I thought I had been transported back home where this was a regular morning question for my wife.

"Yes" I said already anticipating the next line.

"Well you managed to snore through it".

My snozzle is an expensive anti snoring device that I like to believe works perfectly; apparently not.

We decided to skip the unappealing, overpriced breakfast option and head back onto the Stewart Highway, heading north. We returned to our cut off point at Meziadin junction where I could fuel up and we could have breakfast. A girl had pointed out the restaurant the night before, so I urged Wilson to go check it out. He came back to tell me that there was nothing there. We checked with a nearby trucker who said

"Yip it's there and it's darn good".

The entrance was an unmarked door, and the waitress was a first nation's girl with a wonderfully dry sense of humour who clearly didn't give a shit. I liked her. The service was incredibly slow, with Wilson's dish arriving well before mine, but as usual I still finished before him. I can imagine rich tourists complain about the staff, the service etc. but not us. It felt real and we loved it.

Then we continued north through this vast wild country. I pulled over a few times to take some photos, but more importantly just to take in the atmosphere. I was beginning to feel that I was in real wilderness again, just as I had felt in Patagonia. There was so little traffic that I found myself giving trucks a wave as I would do with fellow bikers.

I later met up with Wilson, and we stopped off at a first nations store for fuel and food. It was very basic but had all the essential provisions, and a small coffee and nachos area, with a TV blaring in the background. We continued on, each riding at our own pace, enjoying the road. We had both sighted some black bears scurrying into the undergrowth, avoiding the biker paparazzi. I was only 10 miles from the Alaska Highway junction at Upper Laird when I saw my second grizzly bear grazing at the side of the road. I pulled up a few hundred yards further on and again scrambled to get my camera out. As before my heart was pounding at being in the presence of this magnificent and dangerous animal. Thankfully I got a good shot, and quickly moved on. What a privilege it was to see two wild grizzly bears on this magnificent route.

My final stop on the highway was a pee stop. Having so recently spotted the last giant bear, I felt some trepidation. When I pulled over I tooted my horn a few times, took a serious look around and clapped my hands enthusiastically as I walked to the edge of the woods. I was happily relieving myself when I heard a rumble close by. The blood started to drain from me, until I realised it was the noise of a distant car approaching. A seriously scary moment all the same.

I arrived soon after in Watson's Lake where Wilson was waiting by the famous Sign Post Forest which was started by a bored Soldier putting up a signpost pointing to his home town of Danville, Illinois. As others have added their own signs to it over the years, it has grown into a major tourist attraction. I had a photo taken beside an Eindhoven sign, appropriate as it was somewhere I had worked for 4 years.

"The Sign Post Forest, Watson Lake, Yukon Territory, Canada"

Wilson had already checked out a hotel we had identified, but it was expensive. We checked out the nearby campsite, but it did not appeal. I mentioned that I had seen a motel/pub on my way into town.

"That grotty place?" he said

"Yip" I said "possibly affordable"

It turned out the rooms were actually unaffordable, but at $10 a camp pitch was. There were no facilities other than the pub restaurant, which turned out to be a gem of a find. Its speciality was Schnitzel, which is traditionally pork covered in breadcrumbs. It would not be my natural choice but Wilson assured me it should be good. It was very good, and combined with a great local draught beer we had struck gold.

The restaurant was run by a very pleasant woman in her thirties, with a fearsome looking mother who was hanging out and drinking wine. She shouted loudly at me as I almost used the not at all well signposted lady's toilet. We had a long and jovial chat with a couple of doctors before calling it a night.

When it came time to pay up the host advised us that since we had used the restaurant the camping would be free. We assured her we would be back on our southward journey.

It was on that morning, a further few hundred miles north, that Raymond had entered Alaska just south of Tok.

"Raymond makes Alaska"

Sat 23/5/15

As per our new routine I was up and ready first, and moved on towards a breakfast place that had been recommended the night before. It was forty minutes in the direction of our next destination of Whitehorse. It turned out to be a good recommendation serving wholesome food at local prices. The ride that day was shorter than we had been used to, but still the Yukon threw in some gravel roadworks and a long front wheel wobbling metal bridge to keep me alert. There's a sign post at each of these metal bridges, basically showing a motorcyclist wobbling out of control. I think Canada needs to take a look at this metal/wooden bridge construction issue.

Whitehorse itself was a bit disappointing in that we were expecting more of a frontier town. The town has a population of around 33,000 which is 80% of the population of the vast Yukon Territory. Still lots of wilderness here. We called in at McDonalds to get Wi-Fi and a coffee. I went in for the drinks and when I came back out Wilson was chatting to an old guy who had a three wheeled Cam-Am trike with a stuffed Panda as pillion. Apparently Leo has been riding for 60 years and has had the Panda for 40 years. He was a modest guy, but we somehow found out that he was the face of Canada's bestselling Amber Ale. He directed us to the campsite and told us to come back later when he would take us down to the Yukon Brewery shop.

"Leo - the face of Arctic Red"

We did just that, and came back two up on Wilson's bike. Leo was patiently waiting and led us about a mile or so through town to the brewery shop. The Canadians and apparently north west USA have this brilliant system where you can buy draft ale in a jug they call a Growler, which you then reuse. It's a bit like the draft pack they had in the eighties in Scotland, but much cooler. It's a concept that definitely should come to the UK. Anyway as we were not equipped to carry a Growler, we picked a six pack each. Leo offered to get them for us, but we firmly declined. What he didn't explain was that as a former "face of beer" he was on a free beer for life deal. We later wished he had made that more clear! We stopped off at his house briefly, then went back and had an early night listening to the pleasing sound of a live country band playing on the edge of the campsite. It was a fundraiser for some local musician and a very civilised gathering.

Sun 24/5/15

I was looking forward to visiting Dawson City, with its gold mining heritage. I woke early once again, and rode ahead of Wilson, and again had a couple of gnarly roadworks to deal with. The Yukon is both massive and remote, and there were many miles of wilderness between the small settlements there. My first fuel stop was at a place run by a white bearded (it's the norm up here) guy who had an old Russian sidecar. The second food stop was at a little store where I ended up in conversation with a man who was looking for his dog. This friendly man turned out to be the Chief of the local First Nation of Nacho Nyak Dun. He was part Irish and explained how he had been forced into a boarding school along with all the other First Nation kids. So many wrongs committed by so many people to indigenous natives over the years. I liked him a lot.

Wilson caught up with me just outside of Dawson City and we rode into town together. It was as we had hoped for, an old western looking town: we were directed to a campsite across the Yukon River via a ferry by a helpful Tourist Information officer. The ferry was free, ran 24 x 7 and you could walk into town. I loved the fact we were crossing, yet staying right by, the Yukon River. There is always something very wild and free for me in the name 'Yukon'. We boarded the ferry and made the short crossing. As the ferry pulled in, the captain made an error resulting in a hard bump against the shore, sending Wilson and I down like a deck of cards. The crew rushed over to help us lift the bikes. Luckily we were about a foot away from landing on top of each other. There was no obvious damage so we moved on.

"The Yukon Ferry, Dawson City"

We set up camp, then went back across to the town where we had a great dinner followed by a visit to the casino and a traditional old time western show. I was a bit reluctant, but at just $11 I was not going to be a party pooper. It was actually quite good fun, and in an old fashioned way, entertaining. We then went to do the Sour Toe Challenge. This is where you drink a shot from a glass containing an alleged frost bitten toe from a miner who died in the 1800's. We picked a really bad time as a bus tour party had just beaten us to it, across the road from the Casino. Finally it was our turn and after making sure that we obeyed the rule that the toe has to touch your lips we were initiated by the Captain and joined the elite club of those who had completed the challenge.

Alaska

Route Map

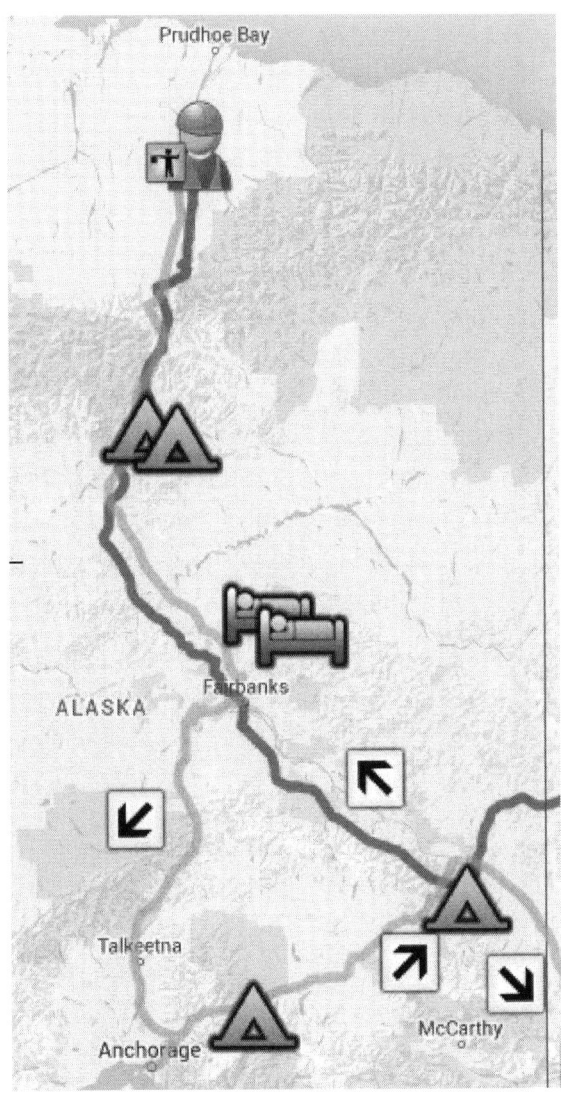

Mon 25/5/15

I woke up to the roar of the fast flowing Yukon River, and the birds chirping. What an idyllic place to spend the night. For reasons unknown it occurred to me that the road to Alaska could be on our side of the river, eliminating the need to take the mad ferry. It turned out that I was right. I wondered about my fuel situation but with my two Rotopax and Wilson following behind at some point, I was sure I would be ok. So with Mr Hutch still soundly asleep I was off to Alaska.

The paved road hardly lasted at all, and despite assurances from the girl on the ferry last night it was 90% gravel all the way to the border. The top of the World Highway was along mountain ridges and it was spectacular in the morning sunshine. The gravel was mainly good with some exceptions on corners. I did have to use my Rotopax before the border but that would be enough as long as there was fuel at the next town, amusingly named Chicken. The border was sign posted as the most northerly land border to the USA. The border guard was pleasant and could sense my elation as I made my target "Argentina to Alaska".

"We made it to Alaska"

He was a biker in hibernation himself and happily took photos for me. I advised him Wilson would be following behind shortly.

Alaska greeted me with perfect tarmac for 5 miles, then good quality gravel all the way to Chicken. I found the only restaurant, which was in a Porto cabin, where a young girl served and cooked the food alone. Still it didn't stop her smiling and 'rasling up' bacon and eggs as she put it. She sent me to the store for coffee, since it was free there. Thankfully there was also gas at Chicken, so I was good to go all the way to the next place, named Tok, which was the town where Raymond had turned south.

I had lunch in Tok, in a traditional American restaurant, then headed along the road for more gas. As I filled up a woman in her fifties was standing nearby, screaming and swearing at her dogs. She noticed me looking at her and barked out aggressively

"Where you from then?"

"Scotland" I replied nervously, hoping to soften her with a friendly smile.

She softened immediately and said sweetly

"Welcome to Alaska"

I smiled when I read a sign just above the cashier as I paid for my gas.

"Welcome to Alaska just north of sanity".

Wilson found me at a gas station, and we agreed we would push on to Fairbanks, some 209 miles north. We eventually arrived in Fairbanks, and were initially unimpressed with what looked like a concrete box town. We did our usual and rode to the BMW dealership, then spied a Super 8 motel close by. I had always considered Fairbanks as basecamp in our push to Prudhoe Bay. We were still hoping for a Friday opening of the Dalton Highway, so we checked in for two nights. We wandered over to some restaurants but found them either very quiet or closed. It had not dawned on us that this was a Memorial Day.

Tues 26/5/15

We had a disturbed sleep that night with some pathetic guy outside pleading with his wife or partner to let him into their room. The pathetic part was when he started what sounded like mock crying. I felt like shouting "no wonder she won't let you in" but with American Gun Laws being what they are, we called reception to deal with him. Next morning we got a change of room to make sure it did not repeat.

We checked out the highway situation but there was still nothing new posted since the last update of the 22nd of May. We rode up to the BMW dealership which also happened to do Harley, Victory, Honda and Polaris, the place was massive. The girl at the service reception was initially kind of hostile, but began to warm to us. Wilson was looking to have his rear brake pads checked and probably replaced. "Your bike has to be clean" she barked, "if not its $30 more".

She directed us to a car wash a few miles away, which we gratefully visited. We each hosed our bikes down for $3 each, and headed back.

The initially grumpy girl was now gone, replaced by a guy. Wilson had decided to go for the brake replacement, a reasonable half-hour' labour. I took him on the pillion back to the hotel for a while, returning him to the dealership a couple of hours later. While we were there we both agreed on a great present for Stevie the mechanic back in Scotland. It was a BMW beanie hat with Trails End Alaska imprinted on it. I was sure he would like it.

I was determined to change Boris's oil and filter again, so I popped into a Walgreens Auto and found the right oil. I then went into a huge Fred Meyers supermarket and purchased a basin to catch the oil. Wilson met me back at the hotel, as I was about to drop the oil in a corner of the car park.

"Maybe not the best place pal" he quite rightly said. "Let's see if we can do it in an Auto-lube place?"

I reluctantly agreed, and we rode up the street to Sears Auto. I went inside and explained that I wanted to change my own oil and asked if they would dispose of it for me. No problem, the guy said. Not sure he realised I was going to do the job in the corner of their parking lot. Anyway I got the job done and Wilson did a nuts and bolts check on both bikes. A satisfying day all round.

That night was spent in Coyote Jack's drinking beer and chatting to the friendly co-owner about life in Alaska. The reoccurring theme is one of characterful people coming north to escape something or other, and liking it. On our return we met a nice guy called Brian that night in reception who in his late sixties was touring the country on a BMW K1600 Side Car outfit. It was an impressive set up and even included a tow bar for a trailer if required.

Wed 27/5/15

Our first task of the day was to check if there was an update on the Dalton situation and the news was not good. The highway was closed with a new estimated opening date of the 5th of June. It said that even if it did open then, it would be single lane and difficult conditions.

It was now clear that we were not going to Prudhoe Bay, as not only would it put our return arrival date at serious risk, it would mean sitting around for days.

Wilson began to enthusiastically describe how he fancied taking the inner passage ferry back down and perhaps catch an early flight home. He still wanted to go to the Arctic Circle first. He tried to engage with me about these ideas, but I had to admit I felt an immense sense of defeat, and at this point did not want to discuss going south.

I told him I would head north and leave him to sort out what he wanted to do. There were no bad feelings between us, it was just how I was feeling. Then I took off, with Coldfoot (my base camp 1) as a destination. I would meet Wilson before the Arctic Circle, and we would celebrate that as a fantastic achievement, and take a Deafblind Scotland picture.

I heeded the warning from the Harley shop girl about massive pot holes and slimy surfaces as I rode north. The pot holes were indeed massive, and I'm glad she had alerted me to them. Sometimes half the road was unpassable.

I stopped off at the Arctic Circle Gift Shop which served free coffee and sold tasty muffins. To my delight it also sold "I have crossed the Arctic Circle" stickers. I met Brian on the Beemer outfit from the night before and he asked me if I was being a little presumptuous buying them now.

"No" I said smiling "I'm doing it at any cost"

He decided not to buy them, and then laughed when he saw the existing Arctic Circle sticker already on Boris.

"Ah, you're already a fraud" he said.

"No sir, been there and done it, in Norway" I replied proudly.

We more or less left together, and he caught up with me when I was crawling through the newly laid slime on the first stage of the Dalton Highway. Fortunately it didn't last long and we were soon on good gravel. We both pulled into a layby for a rest. We had seen a sign saying the Yukon River Bridge was to close for 4-6 hours that day. The guy at the gift shop had advised us food and fuel were on the other side of the bridge, then it was a sixty mile ride to the Circle. A guide with a minibus full of tourists advised us they had been turned back an hour ago, so it would likely be closed for at least three hours more. We messed about a bit but then agreed we would go see.

"Brian and I on the Dalton"

I did not care if it was 6 hours, there was no turning back for me. Brian was more hesitant, but followed on anyway. We rode for about an hour to the bridge, and to our delight we whizzed straight across this impressive wood surfaced structure. We pulled into the Yukon River Camp, and ordered some food to celebrate. Within minutes Wilson joined us, and told me he had booked his sailing for June 1st, and that he would try and pull his flight forward too. He was in good spirits and was keen also to stay in Coldfoot that night. To be honest I was in better spirits by then also. I had reconciled within myself that I could not beat nature, but I could ride up to the final point where nature would beat me.

A further 60 or so miles north, Wilson, Brian and I celebrated having reached the Arctic Circle on our own bikes.

Brian took some great shots of us with the Deafblind Scotland banner. I was particularly heartened to hear Brian say that if it wasn't for us guys, he would have turned back before now. It was a pleasure to celebrate this moment with him. He was heading south now, while Wilson and I rode the next 60 miles to Coldfoot. As usual Wilson sprinted ahead, and by the time I arrived he had arranged free camping across from the restaurant. It was a proper rugged Ice Road Truckers stop, and I loved it. That night we were told the road was closed at a place called Happy Valley, some 150 miles further north. I told Wilson I had to do it, and he told me he didn't.

The two amigos were about to go their separate ways. We both felt good about our plans, so we sank a few beers in recognition of our last night together.

"Celebrating at the Arctic Circle"

Thu 28/5/15

I woke up at 5am to the sound of a truck engine idling. As quietly as I could, I got my bike gear organized, then went over to the restaurant for a breakfast muffin. It was expensive, took forever and tasted bad. I was concerned about my fuel, so I borrowed (stole) Wilson's extra pack, as I knew he would now not need it. I left a note on his bike to thank him, and wish him a safe journey home. I glanced over at his tent as I pulled away, and reflected on the last 4 months together. We had experienced so much in such a short time, and ultimately we had made it to Alaska. I was riding solo from now on, and I was looking forward to this final chapter.

I felt a huge sense of apprehension that cloudy morning, as I pulled out of the muddy car park on my final journey north. What was this road going to be like, had I enough fuel, what if I fell or broke down? Thankfully, at least initially, the Dalton was paved, and the scenery was spectacular as I embarked on my ride into the wilderness. After 35 miles I was greeted by the dreaded 'pavement ends' sign, which made me draw a sharp intake of breath. To be honest the gravel was pretty good, and I made excellent progress towards the looming Brooks Mountain Range.

"The Dalton Highway"

I stopped off for a toilet break in one of the rest areas provided. By this stage I always scoured the area for bears first, before dismounting to do my stuff. I have become slightly nervous when I open the toilet door that a bear has made it in before me, or might be waiting for me when I'm done.

The Brooks Mountain range is famous for challenging the Ice Road Truckers, but on this occasion the road was ice free, though there was snow at the side of the road. There was a steep ascent and descent with good views from the top, but also thankfully all good gravel. I made my way gingerly down the steeper slopes into the valley beyond, which greeted me with more tarmac. I was excited about the prospect of this possibly lasting all the way, but was soon disappointed when it ended just a few miles further north. What greeted me next was horrible pebbly gravel, which lasted for quite a while before leveling out.

I met a Pipeline Security Truck and the driver told me that the closure was still some sixty miles away and that's there was a slime laying operation a few miles ahead. He didn't call it slime, but I knew it was slime as I had experienced it at the start of the Dalton. "That's it" I said to myself "I should turn back now; it totally makes sense". "You can't" said the little voice in my head, "you have to get to the trails end". I cursed that little voice, but I knew it was more powerful than me. The slime laying truck was there as warned, and I nervously crawled through it without falling. Beyond that the surface was not too bad, but the road went on forever. I looked at the deep ditches at the side of the road, and thought what if I crashed and got injured or stuck under the bike? I can imagine the horror of hearing a hungry bear or wolf pack approaching.

"Focus" I said to myself.

I met a second security truck who told me I could not go much further.

"I know" I told him and asked "how much further is it?"

"About 40 miles" was the cruel reply.

I pushed on and on and eventually, a little earlier than he had predicted, I finally spotted some barriers. I had reached the end of the trail. There was no screaming in the helmet this time, just a deep down sense of relief that I had made it. Happy Valley was a featureless valley in the tundra, with an airstrip and lots of construction vehicles. Its name did not seem to fit with its reality.

I took my pictures, fueled Boris from all three containers, and started on the long journey back. It seemed to pass quicker as return journeys often do, except for the last 50 miles or so which were ridden in very heavy rain. Nature was never going to let me say this wasn't an adventure. The round trip turned out to be 320 miles of which 80 miles was tarmac so I was completely exhausted when I made it back to camp that night.

"Trails End "

As expected Wilson had moved south on his journey home. I felt a sense of sadness seeing my tent there on its own on the sodden permafrost ground. Wilson had left me his spare tyre pump and a nice note wishing me all the best.

I had a quick snack with orange juice in the restaurant, and was in tucked up in my sleeping bag before 8pm. I slept well that night, exhausted but knowing in my heart I had done all I could. I had ridden to the end of the trail. I smiled in my sleep.

Fri 29/5/15

The sky was grey and overcast, but at least it was dry that morning. I could feel the effect of the permafrost as soon as I moved off my thermorest, the ground was freezing. I wondered how Wilson had coped with it. He had once felt frozen to death on a camping trip to Durness, in Scotland. Wilson and Raymond are winter gloves, heated grips kind of men. He never mentioned it, so I guess he has hardened to the camping experience. I packed up quickly, certain that rain was not far away. I was not going to use the restaurant for breakfast after yesterday's experience, but did have a coffee and sent a postcard to Amber and my parents.

I had it in my head it was 60 miles to the breakfast stop at the Yukon Bridge Camp, but it was actually 60 miles to the Arctic Circle, then a further 60 miles to the camp. I thought of Brian and Wilson as I passed the Arctic Circle, and their excitement about getting there. It seemed like a long road to breakfast and there was a bit more gravel than expected, but eventually I could see the impressive structure of the bridge and was finally there.

After sharing my breakfast space with some surly road workers and a nice German couple, I was ready to move on. The road beyond was pretty intense as there was recently laid black slime. I took it very easy, but it was not a comfortable ride. I was to learn later that Wilson had come upon it just as it was laid the day before, and had ended up trapped under Ludwig for a bit. Very dangerous stuff for bikes. They need to look at that.

I stopped off again at the Arctic Circle Gift shop, where I had met Brian before. The owners were out, but they had left a man in charge who was the font of all knowledge. The German couple from the Yukon Camp were there and were receiving a lecture on local history. He was a bit eccentric, but I liked him. He explained how my end of the road Happy Valley got its name. Apparently there was a better camp further south for the workers during the construction of the pipeline. Nobody wanted to stay at the bleak camp further north. The solution was to call the bleak camp Happy Valley to attract he workers in.

After negotiating the giant pot holes, I arrived back in Fairbanks, and checked into the familiar Super 8 Motel. I winced at the price, now having no-one to split the bill with. I had just missed Wilson by an hour as he had stayed over the previous night. He was now ferry bound. I took a ride up to the bike shop, and updated the lady there on how far north I had managed to get. From there it was time for an early night and enjoying the facilities of the room.

On checking my email Wilson had mailed me warning me of the fresh slime, and recounting how he ended up under his bike. He also sent through a photo of the washed out Dalton above Happy Valley. I now understood just how serious the closure had been.

"The washed out Dalton Highway"

Sat 30/5/15

I felt a sense of relaxation and familiarity when I awoke that morning. I was able to connect with Amber and also my younger son Liam. I explained that I was flying solo and wanted to make the most of the final two weeks. Amber actively encouraged me to do so, saying "when you're home, you're home". I planned to wash the Dalton grime off my bike that morning but unfortunately could not find my way to the wash station we had used during our last stay.

Before I knew it I was heading out of town towards Anchorage. I stopped quite soon for fuel and water, then made a long ride across a beautiful ridge towards Denali National Park. I initially pulled over at a swanky tourist hotel, but soon found a more modest but touristy row of stores. A Subway was advertised on the side of a building, but before I came to it I stumbled upon the Black Bear Cafe. It was a gem of a place with great coffee, and a nice slice of apple pie. I chatted to a local pilot who also had a Beemer, as I sipped my coffee in the sun. I asked him if I needed to ride into the park to see Delani (Mt McKinley) North America's highest mountain, I was told no, I would have great views a little further down the road. I was delighted as the park looked busy with camper vans and was not drawing me in at all.

I soon stopped at a great spot and took pictures of the majestic mountain which was over 20,000 feet. I recalled how old Boris had climbed up to nearly 16,000 feet in Chile and smiled at the thought. Pulling over at a cafe/store in a place called Beaver Creek I was instantly met by a girl covered in oil, whom I guessed was the waitress. My hello was met with a long dead pan stare. As I wondered what to do a pregnant young girl, looking a bit like a hill billy, came up and showed me to a table. I ordered the burger from a tattooed lady, with some slight concern over its quality. While I was waiting yet another girl carried in a large beetle, with claws, offering to show it to everyone, before taking it into the kitchen. They were actually all nice people, and I know enough not to be fooled by looks, but it was definitely not my most comfortable experience food wise.

I continued on towards Anchorage looking for a campsite along the way; it never materialised. Before I knew it I was in Alaska's biggest city, and not feeling good about it. It looked ok on the surface, but I did not want to be forced into a hotel. I wheeled around the city centre, fuelled up and was then told by a grumpy attendant there was no camping nearby. I decided to head back east, and as luck would have it I stumbled on the Foxes Den RV and Campsite. I was sorted for the night.

As I unpacked I was approached by a chatty man in his sixties.

"You have a missing badge" he drawled.

"What's that?" I asked.

"Route 66" he answered.

"It's a great road" I said and one that I've been on, but not completed, there are no false badges on Boris. He told me how he camps up here every year to chill out and go fishing. Another of Alaska's characterful escapees.

Sun 31/5/15

I awoke reasonably early, and hungry as I had missed dinner the night before. I packed up and headed straight onto Highway 1 North. I had to head north to make my way across to Canada, before turning south. Within minutes of my departure I spotted the Noisy Goose Café, which looked kind of busy for 8am on a Sunday. I pulled over and was not disappointed; the menu, service and atmosphere were first class. A big difference from yesterday's joint.

The road north was more mountainous and interesting than I thought, and I was surprised to stumble upon the Matanuska Glacier. I stopped to take a look and some photos, I noticed I was feeling very relaxed now. At another stop further on, a Coffee Hut at the junction of Highway 1 and 4, the woman recommended I try the local Copper River Sockeye Salmon with salad, on a sandwich. I would never have chosen it, but went with it and man was it delicious. Having me sat outside seemed to draw in a few more customers, so I enjoyed some time out people watching. Shame on that lazy fat guy who sat in his pick-up truck while his wife did all the running.

From there I headed back to Tok, the place we had passed earlier whilst heading for Fairbanks. I stopped off for gas and took the opportunity to hose the Dalton grime from Boris. I would normally be fine with the dirt, but I worried about the grime getting into my brakes etc. I asked the gas attendant lady about camping towards Canada, and she said there were two free sites some fifty miles further on, adding that she would choose the second one. I thanked her and said I would give that a go.

While riding through town I remembered that Wilson had left an expensive under jacket at a restaurant there. He had called them later and said he would pick it up, but with his change of plan I reckoned he would have forgotten about it. It would have been a hell of a detour for him, so I decided to check if it was there and take it with me if it was. The woman knew what I was talking about straight away, and handed it over without fuss. From there I called in at a grocery store and ended up with a salami stick and Pringles (I have to stop doing this) then headed off.

The first campsite appeared, and sure enough a few miles on there was a second. Dead Man's Lake was not a great name - actually it was a great name, for a horror movie. I rode just over a mile down a dirt track and found it was just perfect. Pitch 5 was in the trees, facing the lake, with a toilet block in easy reach.

"The perfect pitch – Dead Man's Lake, Alaska"

I had a great night, chilling and finishing off the Isle of Jura whisky that Amber had bought me for my birthday. I chatted to the elderly Swiss couple who were looking after the site, and listened to the shrill screams of a party of youngsters far off on the other side of the campsite. Tomorrow I would head back to Whitehorse, to that good campsite we had used before, where I would shower and use McDonalds Wi-Fi. I had a plan.

Mon 01/6/15

I awoke to the sound of gentle rain on my tent. Yikes I thought, I hadn't planned for that. I peered out of the tent, seeing how very grey it looked overhead. Could be worse, I thought, the dead man might have risen from the lake and pulled me in. Still I was concerned that my perfect camping plan for the next couple of days could now be at risk. The thing with camping in the wet with a bike is you go in wet, and come out wet; it's not pleasant.

The first priority was to get packed as quickly as I could. I used the picnic table as a shelter for my stuff as I quickly put the tent away. The rain started to come down harder just as I pulled away from the campsite.

Oh my god it's June, I said to myself. It felt strange to be so close to the end of the trip. It felt as if I had been away forever. No 'my holiday flew in' feelings, no 'it was too short feelings' and no 'it was too long' feelings. That has to be a good thing.

I rode towards the Canadian border hoping I might get a chance to spend the last of my dollars. A top up of gas and a breakfast would be ideal. The right place did appear just before the border but as it was only 6:30am, it was closed. Having given up on the dollars spending idea, I left the USA and Alaska, riding the last 20 miles to the Canadian customs post. As it was still raining hard I pulled a little past the window to park my bike in the dry.

"Don't pass this window in future" shouted the customs guy angrily.

I gave my apologies and before long we were on good terms; he was a biker too. Within a few minutes I had completed my final border crossing of the trip and was straight onto crumbling Canadian roads.

The border guy told me that Buckshot Betty's was the place for breakfast, 3 kilometres up the road. It turned out to be fine, not great, but served the purpose. While I was there a biker from Vancouver told me that the road from here to Hayes Junction was full of shit gravel roadworks. I fuelled up and hit the road. It did have some long stretches of gravel, but not such shit gravel. Still it was a pain in combination with the rain. After about 100 miles the roadworks stopped, and the sun came out. I was even blessed by the sighting of another grizzly, grazing at the side of the road. This one was golden in colour, but too quick for the camera this time. There was a ditch which he disappeared into, that ditch led along the road towards me. I was prompted to take off and ride half a mile further on without even putting my gloves back on. You don't mess with the bears.

I stopped off for a coffee at a little outpost called Destruction Bay, another superb name. Turns out a storm wrecked both US and Canadian army camps there a while back. Continuing south east I finally rolled into Whitehorse, which felt totally familiar. I went straight to the campsite from last time, and set up my tent. Grabbing my toilet bag and towel I headed over for a shower, only to discover the toilet block was closed. So I headed back into town to McDonald's for a coffee and Wi-Fi session, and to see if I could spot Leo, unfortunately he was not around. After that it was back to the campsite to rest, write and to have that very welcome shower now that normal service had been restored.

As I messed around near my tent, I was approached by a guy who looked of similar age to me. He asked if I had done the Dempster, another iconic Arctic Circle highway to the north of Canada. He was cycling and had been hearing scare stories about its condition. I explained that I had not done the Dempster, but the Dalton. I advised him about the slime and gravel, but ended with "you have to go for it". He smiled and said that's exactly what he needed to hear, something positive. He asked how things were going, how it was travelling on my own and I explained it was going very well and a bit about the background. He also enjoyed a mix of travelling with friends and going solo, it worked well for him. It was a nice, genuine, human encounter.

Tues 2/6/15

The first item on the agenda next morning was another trip to McDonalds for breakfast and a Wi-Fi catch-up. Leaving McDonald's, I said hi to a guy with a bright yellow Honda Goldwing. He was living in Anchorage, and taking a trip home to Denver, Colorado. I took off before him, but ended up meeting him a couple more times at stops along the way. We would be on the same route for the next few days and I got the distinct impression that he would have liked to team up. To be honest I was enjoying my alone time, especially on the road, so I dodged it, hoping he was not too offended.

The road to Watson Lake was familiar by now, so I knew to expect some roadworks, short gravel sections and that horrible long metal surfaced bridge.

I pulled into the Upper Laird Lodge, where we had previously stayed. I was excited about the prospect of free camping and great food. It was the mother, Goldie who was serving.

"Ah you were the nice guys who returned your wine glasses and trash" she said.

I guess most people don't borrow their wine glasses, but if they did I can't comprehend why they wouldn't return them, and clear up any trash.

I pitched up and took my time getting my gear organised. Walking over to the restaurant I left my iPad to charge, then went for a wander around. Finally I headed back and asked Goldie for a beer. As I remembered from our last visit, she is a bit of a character and she barked at me

"I'm preparing food; I don't have time".

Then, despite my request for a dark beer she threw a lager at me. I sat out on the patio and was soon joined by another guy, who had been clearing trees.

"You enjoying your camp?" he asked.

"Yes it's perfect" I said.

He was soon joined by another three guys. They all looked like raw, Yukon types, with lots of facial hair, baseball caps and tattoo's. I enjoyed listening to them talking about Chevrolets, fishing and tree felling. I moved closer just to get out of the sun, but they asked me to join them.

They were a great set of guys, except maybe for the quiet, mean looking one who was clearly unsure of me. After a while I went inside, and discovered Goldie was cook for the night. I guess if she had taught her daughter, she had to be good too, so I ordered the special rib-eye and it was delicious. While I was there a tall gangly guy with a deep voice came in with a girl.

"You like your campsite?" he drawled.

"It's great" I replied, now getting a little concerned that everyone in Watson Lake knew about my tent in the woods. It turned out the two of them were on a first date and I was fully entertained as I could not avoid overhearing their conversation. He was loud, worked as a mechanic and fixed anything. He was a man's man and had no social graces. She sounded Eastern European and was much quieter and seemed reserved. A guy came in at one point and asked him about car parts.

"I'll come and pop the hood" he declared and left for twenty minutes.

At some point they were having a discussion about food. She said very emotionally that it's important to her because she was starved as a child. His response? "Get over it".

As they left to continue their new relationship, I also left to go sleep.

Wed 3/6/15

I took the advice of the boys from the night before and did breakfast at Bee Jays on the outskirts of town. It was a restaurant come garage, and a bit basic. I had the basic breakfast, then wandered along to the workshop. I asked the guys if they had an extra tyre valve cover, as I had lost mine. I noticed the surly guy from the night before, despite my attempt at a friendly greeting, he remained the surly guy. I had a good result though, as the cheery garage guy handed me a valve cover, and I was on my way.

I was expecting a boring ride to Fort Nelson but was in for a surprise as I hit some cracking scenery at Mundo Lake in the Northern Rockies. The weather did eventually turn very bad for the boring third part of the journey, so I was glad when I finally reached Fort Nelson. The town itself looked dreary in the rain as I pulled off into the tourist information centre. It turned out to be a great stop with Wi-Fi, free coffee and good service. I took a list of hotels and headed on through town to make a choice. I ended up picking the Fort Nelson Hotel where I was able to negotiate a corporate rate of £55. It was a 'stay in' night, taking full advantage of the comfortable bed and TV.

Thu 4//6/15

As I had the luxury of a hotel, I decided to take my time that morning. For me taking my time was a 9am start, rather than 7am. There were still clouds in the sky and puddles of water in the parking lot but it was dry overhead. I had a vision of the scenery en-route to Dawson Creek being good, just like yesterday, however just as yesterday surprised me with good, today surprised me with bad. Other than a good bear encounter it was like riding through Finland, all road and trees. It seemed very much like a trucker's route and sadly I seemed to be heading towards civilisation with more and more habitations showing up.

There was one highlight however, and that was an impromptu stop at the Taylor tourist information centre. The lady there was Portuguese and she treated me wonderfully well. First, she fed me cupcakes, left over from a recent open day, then brewed fresh coffee. She then took ages explaining where I should go and what I should do.

I did take her advice to divert off the highway, picking up a little bit of the old Alaskan highway and carefully crossing the last remaining bridge constructed of wood.

Dawson Creek was a bit industrial looking, but my lady had recommended the Mile 0 RV and Campsite which turned out to be ideal. I wandered along the road from there to a proper bar and listened to one of my favourite Country and Western songs, the appropriately titled "I love this bar". I loved that bar.

"Alaska Highway Mile 0 marker, Dawson Creek, Canada"

Fri 5/6/15

I awoke extra early at just before 5am, and made my way over to the toilets to get cleaned up. I remembered most Tim Hortons were open 24 x 7 so I thought that could make a good breakfast stop. I wanted to get to my destination, Jasper, early to make sure I got a camping spot before the weekend warriors arrived. I did not find a Tim Hortons but a McDonalds did just fine.

The road became roadworks two minutes out of town. A horrible ridged surface, and it went on for miles. After that the road became good, and soon I was entering the territory of Alberta. This part of Alberta was green, flat and looked nice. It continued like that for a while before the roadworks descended on me again. Reaching the town of Grande Prairie, which was bigger than I expected, I fuelled up ready for the "long industrial stretch" that I had been warned about by a biker at a rest stop the previous day. It was full of trucks and oil/forestry activity as described, but it was not too bad. After about 100 miles the snow topped Rockies came in to view and the industry thinned out.

I was just thinking that I had had no animal sightings for a while, when a beautiful young black bear ran across the road in front of me. Result.

I finally made the main route into Jasper and the national park. There were mountains on each side of me, looking like a manicured Glen Coe. What was even more impressive was the turquoise colour of the lakes. Jasper itself was, as expected, a pretty tourist mountain town. I stopped off at the tourist information centre for directions to the campsite which was only 2 kilometres out of town. I got a pitch no problem, camped up then walked into town for a nosey.

Sat 6/6/15

The sun was out as I awoke from a good night's sleep. I showered and sorted my kit out, then took the bike into Jasper. I was amazed that there were some gift shops open even before 8am. I walked to Tim Hortons only to discover a massive queue. I'm not a queue person, so I moved on to a little baker's shop which I had discovered earlier. There was a small queue there too, but more bearable. I then made my way to the visitor's centre looking for Wi-Fi. It was then that I noticed there had been a time zone change; it was an hour later than I had thought.

 After some internet surfing, gift shop browsing and refuelling I made my way back to camp. Then came the long trek back to town on foot, where I settled into the Jasper Brewing Co to watch the champion's league final (Barcelona versus Juventus). It was a great match which Barca won 2-1. From there I did some chilling in the park and headed back, after some dinner, for an early night. Just out of town a couple pulled over in a 4x4 and said,

"Just to let you know we saw a big Grizzly bear on the road where you're heading only 10 minutes ago".

"Ok thanks but that's my only route to the campsite", I said.

"Just thought we would let you know" he said and waved goodbye.

I practiced some risk avoidance by walking on the side of the road rather than through the woods. I also whistled loudly and sang my football team's anthem "I'm Killie till I die". In the end the bear was nowhere to be seen. Perhaps it was enjoying the spectacle from the cover of the trees, who knows?

Sun 7/6/15

I awoke around 5am and popped my head out the tent and saw what I thought at first was a person moving around, but it turned out to be an elk. Then there was not only one elk but a herd, all silently moving through the campsite. It was an amazing sight in the half light. I had never realised they were such big creatures, each the size of a horse. I had noticed a sign in the toilets the previous night saying "Grizzly Bear actively hunting elk calves in this campsite". Thankfully there was no sign of the bear following them.

WARNING

MISE EN GARDE

WHERE:
Whistlers Campground

ENDROIT :
Terrain de camping Whistlers

WHY:
Grizzly bears actively hunting elk calves in the campground

RAISON :
Des grizzlis chassent des nouveau-nés de wapiti dans le terrain de camping.

"Campsite Warning"

I headed back into Jasper, hoping to find breakfast. The only option at that time was Tim Horton's which was fine with me. I then made my way onto Highway 93, the Ice Fields Highway. It was a beautiful ride with the mountains still sporting some snow on top. Again I was struck by the turquoise colour of the rivers and lakes and by the fast speed at which they flowed. I stopped off at one lake where the reflection from the hills was picture perfect.

Next up was the Columbia Ice Field followed by the Athabasca Glacier. All very impressive. I thought about my parent's trip in the mid-eighties as I approached Lake Louise. I remember them proudly describing how beautiful it was, and how much they loved Banff. The lake itself was beautiful but smaller and more closed in than I expected, and in my opinion the hotel that towers over it should be demolished. From there it was onwards to Banff, which was located just off Highway 1, a twin lane highway running all the way from Lake Louise. I did not expect to encounter highways in this area, rather nice twisty single lane mountain roads, so this was a bit disappointing. Banff was modern and touristy, worth seeing, but too expensive for me to stay in.

Here's my theory. On this trip I had become used to raw nature. While this part of the Canadian Rockies was picture postcard perfect, the human influence in highways, towns and facilities is too much. For example naming a tourist stop village Pocohauntos is just over the top. It's a stunning area, worth visiting but.......

I headed back past the Lake Louise turn off, and stayed on highway 1 heading west. I eventually came to a town called Golden and was sent to Mary's Motel by the friendly visitor centre staff. It was a really nice little town and much more real and appealing than either Jasper or Banff had been for me. I must confess I think I could be way in the minority on this.

Mon 8/6/15

I was by now conscious that I did not want to get to Vancouver too early that week. I was still tempted to retrace the Sky to Sea route via Whistler but I had remembered Butch telling me the Canyon (route 1) was good. I had breakfast in a local café close to the hotel, then took off. I had heard on the TV that the road had been closed due to a wreck, but thankfully all was well by the time I got there. I stopped off at a visitor centre in Glacier National Park, which was entertaining and informative. I enjoyed a video advising on how to deal with bears, depending on how the bear was acting. I can only imagine in a real life situation how tense it would be trying to decide if a bear saw you as a meal or a threat.

I left the highway at a town called Revelstoke, to grab a coffee. Again I was pleasantly surprised by what a nice little town it was. From there I continued south, and finally hit Cache Creek. I noticed a campsite on the way in but was not sure, so rode into town without stopping there. I fuelled up then went into a liquor store and asked the guy what my options were. He was very positive about the Brookside campsite I had just passed so I decided to call it a day and make camp there. The lady at reception was friendly and I got a nice pitch in the shade, with a fire pit and bench. I had to ask the caretaker guy to switch off the sprinkler next to me as it was hitting my pitch. He was a biker too and took me up in his little Polaris to collect firewood. I had a great last night of camping, sitting by my fire that night. I had made contact with Kevin, whom we had met on our way up, and he had offered me accommodation at his house. I confirmed I would be with him on Wednesday for one night.

Tues 9/6/15

I unpitched my tent that morning, in the driest conditions of the trip. Not even a drop of moisture on the tent or groundsheet, making for an easy pack. The gods were with me as this would save me the effort of drying out the kit later to get it ready for the trip home. I rode down the canyon, expecting a big highway, but to my delight it was a scenic route which followed the very impressive Frazer River. I'm glad I listened to Butch. I stopped off at another great town called Hope, where they filmed Rambo. It was a great little town with good coffee, and to my further delight, a barber shop. I had a few laughs with the barber and his elderly clientele as he tidied me up.

I finally entered Vancouver, pulling off at the Grandview exit and into the familiar carpark of the 401 motel.

"How much?" I asked despairingly.

"$140" she repeated. "You're lucky we have a cancellation, the women's World Cup is on and the city is full".

"Let me think about it" I said but knew I had little choice.

I checked in and took the time to do my washing and organise my bags then wandered along to the familiar Boston Pizza House for dinner.

Wed 10/6/15

I decided to wash my bike next morning. I used the bin as a bucket, and some washing up liquid I had bought for camping. The other guests looked at me with puzzled expressions as they made their way to work. After that I went in search of breakfast, which was a bit harder to than expected; eventually after a long walk in the hot sun, I found it. I checked out at 11am as required, but spent another hour or so in reception surfing the net and chilling, before making my way out to Richmond and Kevin's Harley dealership. The Sat Nav took me on a short detour, but eventually I found it.

To kill some time, I wandered into the very large Yamaha/Honda/Kawasaki dealership next door. It was great just to wander around and dream about having a multi bike garage. I then headed over to Kevin's Harley dealer and was astonished by the scale of it. It was two stories with a massive apparel department, loads of bikes, a coffee shop and even a games area. I had never been in such a big dealership in my life.

After a while Kevin appeared, he was enthusiastic as ever, and took me on a tour of his shop. I agreed to head to his house and leave him get on with his work.

"Just don't let the cat out" he said with a grin.

It was a 20-minute ride to his town house, and I was relieved to see the garage door rise as I typed in the code. It was an amazing place with a good sized garage on the ground floor, a living/kitchen area on the first floor with a balcony and a couple of bedrooms on the top floor. The cat was great, and thankfully didn't try to get out. Kevin then texted me suggesting we go to a restaurant a walkable distance away that night.

Perfect was my reply. We had a really nice night and I truly appreciated his hospitality.

"Kevin in his garage"

Thurs 11/6/15

Next day I rode the first 10 miles or so with Kevin, before he headed over the bridge to work. As we waved to each other I felt sure we would meet again. I rode with the commuter traffic towards Vancouver eventually turning off for Richmond where the freight company were based. I found Allcargo Express with ease, and asked for Rich. He turned out to be a pleasant middle aged man of Philippine origin. I had to unpack my panniers and sort out what I would take with me and what I would ship. Initially he told me I had to remove my panniers, but as they add very little width to the bike and I persuaded him to leave them on. Rich then ran me to my hotel for my final night in the Americas.

I had booked the Hilton Vancouver Airport on points that I had left over from my working life. It was a modern building close to the station. I revelled in the luxury of my one-bedroom suite taking a hot shower, then sorting out my packing, before walking to the station and heading downtown to take a look at Vancouver. As expected it was a great looking city. I took an elevator up to a revolving restaurant to get a bird's eye view. I had already checked that they do beers only; I did not want overpriced food. I thoroughly enjoyed my overpriced beer with a brilliant view. From there it was a street vendor hot dog and another beer in a nearby Brew Bar.

Fri 12/6/15

I woke up on my last morning of the trip to a windy day. I had already spotted a potential venue for breakfast that would beat hotel prices and made my way there. I could move in slow motion that morning as I had a 12 noon check out, setting me up nicely for the airport.

The shuttle to the airport was shared with an Indian family who were clearly in conflict with each other, judging by the alternating raised voices and tense silences. After check-in I moved through the airport and was again thankful for my previous work status; it meant I was able to get into the Executive Lounge. They all differ but this was one of the best I'd known, with hot meals, delicious sweets and draft beer. Before long it was time to board, and with that, time also to close the trip.

After Thoughts

On my return to Scotland the Three Amigos met up two more times before Raymond flew back home to Sydney. The first was to attend a meeting with East Dunbartonshire's Provost along with Deafblind Scotland. The latter was to do a closing appearance on STV Glasgow. We chatted for a while in the car park after the recording. We all felt the same feeling, that was that, this was the end, it was over and done with. We all felt a sense of loss.

"A chapter ends, never to be forgotten"

I found it pretty difficult to adapt to normal life on my return. As per our discussion in Pasto, Columbia I was always on a mission to get to Alaska, and that drove me forward. I loved riding my bike every day, facing new challenges and experiences. As the main organiser and planner this trip had consumed me for over a year prior to departure. Now that I was back and jobless I felt a lack of purpose. I had moved from being 'funemployed' to unemployed.

I have zero regrets that I made the trip. It was an amazing experience taking me through major highs, lows and everything in-between. I have been challenged physically, intellectually and emotionally on numerous occasions. I have enjoyed the most amazing scenery, witnessed acts of kindness, camaraderie and have been shown great trust by people on the road. Amazingly there were times I never knew what day of the week it was.

I ended up being pretty much spot on with my budget with the overshoot accounted for entirely in accident repairs.

Settling back into relationships has also been a challenge as you will imagine everyone has to go through an adjustment period.

I am pleased to say I am making great progress on all fronts. I am also still actively raising cash for Deafblind Scotland by volunteering (along with Wilson) to do speaking events at local clubs.

So what about man's best friend Boris. Captain Jim, shaking his head, described him in Mexico as the only example of a motorcycle being held together by sticky tape that he had ever encountered. Well you know by now he made it to Alaska despite that high impact shunt in Panama and being thrown down the road in Canada. I enlisted the help of Craig who with his son CJ runs a fantastic old style motorcycle repair shop (Racin & Crusin) in Kirkintilloch. Using a mix of second hand and new parts, Boris has been brought back to a state that I am proud of. He looked after me, I look after him. I am sure we will have more good shared times to come.

Our Just Giving site is still active so please feel to donate to www.justgiving.com/thelongwayuppanamerican

The record of our trip is available on our Facebook Group "The Long Way Up PanAmerican"

I was asked me at a recent speaking event if I would do another trip.

"I imagine it's a bit like having a baby" I said, "You forget the pain quickly".

She mentioned this in her thank you address and invited me to come back when I had my next baby.

I smiled thinking

"I will"

Ride Safe

Top 10 Learnings

1. The way to turn a dream into a reality is to just decide to do it
2. Don't always trust the opinion of others on what lies ahead. Experience it for yourself
3. If you are riding in company, make space for self-time
4. Take time to communicate with people even if you don't have the language
5. Never give up
6. Be careful on Canadian wooden bridges
7. Take large denomination US dollars to Argentina for exchange
8. A smaller free standing tent works best in South America
9. Less is more
10. Don't bring a shaving mirror

Statistics

- Miles Travelled - 22,741
- Oil and Filter Changes - 3 (Peru, Mexico and Alaska)
- Air Filter Changes - 1 (Chile)
- Spark Plugs - 1 set (USA)
- Tyres - 2 sets - (Bolivia, Peru and USA)
- Drive Shaft Gasket – 1 (USA)
- Breakdowns – 0
- Dropped - 4 times (Argentina x 3 / Canada x 1)
- Knocked off – 1 (Panama)

Gear Review

Tent	Robens Voyager 3x	Fantastic tent with luggage space and you can sit inside in the rain. I would recommend a freestanding tent with a smaller footprint for tight Patagonian campsites
Sleeping Bag	Mountain Equipment Titan 450	Perfect even in the Arctic permafrost
Sleeping Mat	Thermorest	Perfect even in the Arctic permafrost
Pillow	Thermorest	Comfortable but bulky to pack versus air pillows
Camping Chair	Helinox	Perfect small pack size, comfortable and lightweight
Waterproof roll-bag	Lumo	Amazing value for money
Torch and Headlight	Petzl	Performed well

Hydration Pack	BMW	Hardly used but worked ok
Camera	Sony Cybershot	Did the job
Helmet cam	GoPro Hero 3 Black	Short battery life encouraged little use
Communication system	Scala Rider G4	Worked really well
Towel	Life Venture Trek XL	Perfect
Laptop / Note-Book	IPad2 / Acer Aspire Switch 10	Worked great
Waterproofs	RevIt	Light to pack but we all had rips - lacks durability
Over Mits	Spada	Great value
Off-Road Boots	SIDI Adventure Gore-Tex Boots	Amazingly comfortable and waterproof - great
Sat Nav	Garmin Zumo 660	Durable in crash but hard to see in sunlight
Stove	Primus Gravity II	Great but hardly used
Helmet	Shark Evoline 2	Love the helmet but had bad fogging issues in

		heavy rain
Suit	BMW Rallye	Saved me in the crash
Gloves	BMW Rallye	Great gloves.
Hard Panniers	Bumot	Without a doubt saved my trip. I love them.
Crash Bars	SW-Motech	Very durable and well tested. I wish I had fitted the upper bars. I have since.

17227217R00134

Printed in Great Britain
by Amazon